RELIGIOUS FAITH, LANGUAGE, AND KNOWLEDGE

Religious Faith, Language, and Knowledge

(A philosophical preface to theology)

BY

BEN F. KIMPEL

Professor of Philosophy, Drew University

PHILOSOPHICAL LIBRARY
NEW YORK

To the Students and Faculty of Drew University

PREFACE

Religious faith is the conviction that there is one reality which is supremely worthy of man's trust, which is therefore neither in human life, nor in the physical world, but is transcendent of both.

Implied in this faith is also the conviction that something of its nature can be known for the trustworthy guidance of human life.

But this faith is discredited by every philosophy which develops out of the premise of Empiricism. According to Empiricism, man can know only his experiences, one type of which is his language. Hence, according to all consistent philosophical empiricisms, in knowing language expressions, one knows only experiences: not informed interpretations of a reality external to experience.

Thus, philosophies of language which begin with the empiricist premise discredit the religious faith that something can be known of a divine reality. Yet, it is safe to say that most contemporary theories of language begin with the empiricist premise, and therefore are anti-theological. But, without a theology, which is an interpretation of the divine reality transcendent of human experience, there is no religious faith.

Contemporary pragmatisms, for example, which constitute one type of Empiricism, maintain that the function of language is simply to facilitate behavior. According to this point of view, language is behavior, and designates only behavior, and the part of our behavior which is experimentally controlled is said to be scientific research. This point of view is Operationism, or Operationalism, according to which, we know only the operations we perform, and nothing more.

The upshot of these popular philosophies of knowledge is a nominalistic theory of language, according to which, we know only language signs. Since language-uses are conventions, the point of view is referred to as Conventionalism, according to which, nothing more is known in science than language conventions.

When language conventions are systematized, we have a grammar, and according to contemporary Logical Empiricism, a knowledge of these conventional rules is the extent of all warranted knowledge-claims. According to this position, we know our statements: and a statement formed according to conventionally accepted rules of grammar is said to be "true". Hence, the only truth of which we may claim knowledge, according to this empiricist analysis of language, is grammatical, or syntactical truth: it is a property of our statements when formed in accordance with the rules of statement-formation. One such system of rules is symbolic logic.

But this current emphasis upon symbolic logic as the norm of language-use is indeed a symptom of our age. It is an expression of a belief that all that can be known for certain are operations upon language: not anything of a reality other than language. This contemporary point of view, however, is not only an expression of belief about what can be known: it is also an expression of disbelief. It is a skepticism toward the warrant for affirming knowledge-claims of a reality transcendent of experience. Hence, it is anti-theological, and so either as a theory of language or as a theory of knowledge, it is irreconcilable with religious faith.

If, therefore, contemporary empiricisms are accepted as the last word in an analysis of language and knowledge, there is no possible way to respect any religious literature as a statement of informed interpretations of a divine reality. What is at stake, consequently, in contemporary empiricist theories of language is not merely an academic problem. If it were, nothing of life and death significance would be involved. What is at stake, is religious life itself.

Religious life is a faith that a knowledge of a divine reality is possible, and one expression of this faith is the use of language to state interpretations of this reality. Religious literature, and religious institutions likewise, express the belief that knowledge of the divine reality can be communicated by means of language for the instruction of all who seek to know a "Wisdom which needing no light, enlightens the minds that need it."

But this cognitive function of language, which is basic to religious life, is repudiated by every empiricist analysis. Unless, therefore, another theory of language can be intelligently defended, statements of religious faith, as well as the educational function of religious institutions, cannot be intelligently defended.

One conviction motivating this essay is that one source of today's skepticism toward religious faith, and religious institutions, is the current empiricist theories of language which enjoy such widespread popularity. Another conviction is that an alternative philosophy of language can be stated which is compatible with the knowledge-claims of religious faith, and which can justify the educational office of religious literature and religious institutions.

PREFACE

Such a philosophy of language must, of course, acknowledge the many sound points of view in the empiricist theories of language and knowledge, without, however, confining either an analysis of language, or of knowledge, to an impiricist point of view.

I should like to acknowledge my gratitude to the President of Drew University, Dr. Fred G. Holloway, and to the members of the Board of Trustees of the University, for granting me a leave of absence during which I wrote this essay. I should also like to acknowledge my indebtedness to Miss Elizabeth Haven of the administrative staff of the University for her generous help in preparing the copy. My most grateful acknowledgment goes to my parents who have provided me with every condition conducive to undisturbed study.

Ben F. Kimpel

Drew University,
Madison, New Jersey.

1

LANGUAGE ANALYSIS AS A MODERN FETISH

AN ALMOST pathological anxiety to save one's self from being accused of error in belief is expressed today in an awesome attitude toward symbolic logic and toward pure mathematics as one development within symbolic logic. Logic and mathematics are regarded by many educated individuals today as they were regarded by Descartes and his followers three hundred years ago. They are looked upon by them as the rock of intellectual security, which above all other human possessions is free from error.

But this widespread attitude not only reveals a desire to avoid error in belief. It also reveals an ignorance of the nature of logic and mathematics.

Mathematics as a strictly formal system is a manipulation of language symbols. It is a substitution of one symbol for another, according to rules of interchange. As a formal system, therefore, mathematical expressions have "sense only", and "no nominata". (1) That is, they name nothing. They are symbols whose meaning can be translated by other symbols, but none of the symbols has significance in referring to any non-symbolic reality. According to this point of view, mathematics is a manipulation of language symbols according to the rules of a

1

specialized language itself, for the purpose only of showing how consistent one can be with his own rules.

That this is a difficult performance, no one would deny. But, when the method of mathematics so conceived is dogmatically declared to be the only philosophical function of language which is entitled to respect, then more than a philosophy of language is involved: the entire character of one's life becomes affected.

If language is not a means for expressing interpretations of reality, and is no more than a means for designating how language is to be used according to a system of rules, then all metaphysical philosophy, including theology, has the status only of a verbal system. But even though every step in a mathematical system may be accounted for by the rules of mathematical grammar, it is certainly dogmatic in the extreme to generalize from this fact to the philosophical principle that language can be accurately used only for purely deductive purposes.

It is, however, essential for an understanding of the nature of some highly specialized developments within mathematics, such as calculus, to recognize that "the symbols of mathematics are . . . symbols either of other symbols or of operations with symbols." (2) That much of mathematics can be accounted for by this interpretation, no one may deny. But that it is an analysis of the nature of *every* aspect of mathematics is another matter.

If for example, an individual extends one finger after another, the order of the sequence is an order in which one event or item is added to another. After these operations have been counted, they constitute a sum, and from this sum, one may in turn take away, or subtract. And further, if there is a unit in terms of which one wants to count this sum, he divides the sum by the unit. These simple operations do not by any means account for the highly specialized developments of mathematics, but the highly specialized developments also do not constitute any evidence whatsoever that non-language operations are not designated by mathematical symbols. (3)

Many mathematical systems, to be sure, cannot be accounted for by any reference to events in daily experience, and that part of mathematics which cannot be traced to elementary activities in daily experience may be explained, as some logicians explain it, as a derivation from logic, or as one instance of the use of pure logic. But, in so far as any connotation of number is derived from the elementary operations of counting, adding, subtracting, and dividing, number itself is not purely a logical rule. It is rather a term whose sense is at least partially derived from non-symbolic, or non-language experience.

A most obvious fact with which one is confronted in the analysis of language is that there were experiences before there were symbols to designate them. It is, therefore, high handed to look back upon life from the vantage point of the most abstract of formal systems, and repudiate any common ancestry in the practical uses of symbolism.

When every branch of learning, therefore, is brought under a single category of symbolism, and all symbolism is assumed to be a manipulating of signs according to rules, then it is obvious that language has only one function in every branch of so-called knowledge. It is a purely analytical function. Every expression in mathematics, in science, in philosophy, and in theology would then be particular instances of the manipulation of language signs according to the rules of language formation. When this interpretation of the nature of symbolism, and the functions of symbolism, trickles down into minds insufficiently acquainted with the phenomena of language itself, it is no wonder that religious beliefs are treated with the same amusement as many sophisticated moderns treat the geometry of Euclid, and the physics of Newton. But when one understands more of the nature of language, and the particular uses to which it was put in the geometry of Euclid, and in the physics of Newton, he is prepared to respect these justifiably time-honored achievements of the human mind, and is also more ready to rethink the function of language in religious life.

As a matter of fact, if all geometries are only a matter of language conventions, and basic to astronomy is such a purely arbitrary geometry, then the sophisticated modern should not speak of Copernicus with such approbation, and should not reject with such finality the astronomy of Ptolemy. For according to a sophisticated philosophy of language, as mere conventional manipulation of signs which point to nothing beyond the signs themselves, it would make no difference whatsoever whether we were to say "the earth rotates", or "the heavens revolve". If there is no criterion by which a language statement must be judged except the rules of language-formation itself, then Ptolemy is every bit as sound as Copernicus, and the much heralded discrediting of Aristotle's cosmology turns out to be not so much a mark of the renaissance of modern thought, as it does to be "much ado about nothing".

One of the serious tasks today confronting an intelligent individual is not only to understand the nature of language with its interpretative function. It is also to develop his capacities for interpreting the complex reality in which he lives, so that even within the limits of language, he may affirm significant propositions. This is not only an academic responsibility. It is also a moral responsibility in the knowledge-quest of human life.

Statements, obviously, which do not conform to the rules of conventional language-formation do not meet the requirements of language-use. But when a statement violates no rule of language, there is no way whatever to invoke a rule of language for discrediting the statement. The only statements which can be discredited by rules of language are statements which violate these rules, and when they do not, an analyst of language has no right to pass judgment upon them, since they are not within his province.

What is within the province of an analyst of language is language, and then only in so far as a particular instance of language either conforms to, or violates, the rules of language formation.

1. *The rules of language stipulate conditions for a statement of thought; not for thinking.*

"The criterion of thinkability" (4), therefore, is not in the possession of any analyst of language. The rules of language stipulate conditions for the statement of thought, and only if there were no thought unless stated in language would the rules of language also stipulate the limits of "thinkability". But rules of language do not perform this function. Their function is much more modest: they stipulate conditions only of expressibility. Expressibility in language, however, is one thing: thinkability is another.

Rules for expressing thought in language-form have developed out of the use of language, but uses of language

5

preceded a formulation of rules. It is therefore a strange inversion of order to suppose that all language which has been developed to express thought, should when formalized into a formal discipline, as logic, or grammar, be cited as the authority by which thought itself is discredited for not confining itself to such forms. Yet, this is just what is proposed when one presumes to pass judgment upon the limits of thinkability by citing the rules of language. Within the purely formal principles of logic, many statements can be made: and it is not possible to ascertain which of these statements is warranted by a criterion other than internal consistency. A statement which contradicts itself must indeed be rejected as illogical, but when a proposition is not self-contradictory, it is not logic, or a method of logical analysis, which may pass judgment upon its warrantability. In other words, by means of the formal rules of logic alone, one is not able to ascertain which statement affirms "a possible state of affairs".

For the individual, therefore, who proposes to use language as a means for expressing an interpretation of a reality other than language, more than grammatical proficiency and logical aptitude are necessary. One must have an interpretation to express, and this requirement cannot be fulfilled by a knowledge of grammar, or by a knowledge of logic.

When it is said, therefore, that "the *only* method of philosophy" is discovering by language analysis "the meaning of propositions" (5), the function of philosophy is so circumscribed that it could never be open to the accusation of error in judgment. Although this prescription of the function of philosophy is a way to save one's face, it is also a way of reducing philosophy to a trivial status in human life.

If, however, one is interested in knowing something about the nature of the context in which he lives, and not only everything about the language he uses, he must employ language for its informative function. Although language may be used to designate the sense of words, it may also be used to state an interpretation of a reality which is other than language. A use of language to state an interpretation of the various orders of existence in which one lives is then indeed contributing to "empirical" knowledge.

2. *Language may state an interpretation of a non-linguistic reality, and so express an empirical knowledge-claim.*

That language may in some way contribute to empirical knowledge is, of course, an assumption. But it is also an assumption that it cannot. If one, therefore, is not to spend his life in this senseless charge and countercharge of dogmatism, he might make real progress in the achievements of knowledge by recognizing that all interpretations express points of view, or are based on presuppositions, and the point of view which one regards as most defensible is the presupposition basic to his philosophy. Everyone who ventures an interpretation, and not merely an affirmation of the sense with which he uses a term, presupposes something not only about language, but also about a reality other than language. When, however, one believes that there is a reality other than language, he is not content to limit himself to an analysis only of language statements. Yet, such limitation is demanded by contemporary theories of language which presuppose the empiricist premise as the one bedrock of philosophical procedure.

3. *What is modern in philosophical analysis is the development of symbolic techniques.*

An emphasis upon an analysis of language is not, however, unique to contemporary philosophy. What is a characteristic of much contemporary philosophy is the insistence that the primary concern in philosophy is the clarification of the meaning of statements, rather than interpreting the nature of a reality other than language. The task of philosophy, therefore, according to much contemporary analysis, is to clarify the meaning of statements, and according to this interpretation, the function of philosophy is purely an operation upon language.

Although everyone is aware that no significant discourse is possible unless there is some common understanding of terms, an agreement, nevertheless, upon terms is something more than a courtesy among individuals who propose to engage in discourse. An agreement upon the sense of a term is also an agreement in the interpretation of some "given", which in non-academic life is very often a non-language reality.

The fertility of the mind, however, in substituting one expression for another was never before as fully appreciated as it has been in the last decades when symbolic logic has required more and more volumes to do it justice. But the very understanding of what symbolic logic proposes to do, makes one aware that an increase of language expressions is not necessarily an extension of the scope of knowledge-claims. An entire logic might be developed by operating upon the sense with which a very few symbols are used in discourse, as for example, a complete analysis of what is meant when one says "work and pray", rather than "work or pray", might itself consume as much space in print as the great *Summa Theologica* of St. Thomas Aquinas.

Whereas, however, Aquinas proposed for his *Summa* the entire range of existence, many modern analysts of language limit the range of their philosophizing to the sense with which a few symbols are used. Thus one noteworthy mark of achievement in language analysis is the ability to say more and more about less and less. According to this ideal of philosophy, the system which could eliminate all but a very few symbols, and so state in terms of these few what had been stated previously by the use of many more, represents the ultimate goal of intellectual achievement.

That this is an achievement, no one would deny. The ability to carry on an extended discourse on the expanded sense of a few symbols is a skill which should not be depreciated. But a skill in reducing the number of terms employed in any discourse should not be construed to be a reduction in the range of reality which confronts an individual interested in interpreting more than symbols.

Symbolic logic is a manifestation of the clarity of thinking which is possible within a very restricted segment of experience. But the range of experience within which symbolic logic achieves its luxuriant growth consists of symbols only, and an analysis of the sense of symbols *in terms of symbols* is symbolic logic. Symbolic logic is one development within language analysis: it is an application of the principles of language analysis to a very restricted range of language. That such restriction is an academic accomplishment no one would deny, and no one would deny that it is a feat of the mind to be able

9

to write copiously upon a fraction of a fragment of experience. But talented as such a demonstration of intelligence is, it is not the only way to manifest intelligence.

If an individual has a highly specialized skill in explicating the sense of a few symbols, the confinement of his talents to this scope of interest is psychologically significant, but not metaphysically significant. The range of an individual's interest is not an index to the range of existence. One might know everything there is to know about a few symbols in language, but such an achievement of intelligence should never pass into a dogmatism which denies the existence of other objects of interest.

If the expanded sense of a symbol is the goal of language analysis, then an analyst should be perfectly clear about what he claims information. His information is about the sense of language signs, and if there were nothing more in existence than such symbols, only a relatively few logicians would possess the much envied warrant to speak authoritatively. But if existence is not exhausted by symbols, then it is unwarranted for anyone to presume that the criterion of philosophical competency is set by the logician.

Life is complex indeed, and there may legitimately be many interests in many different types of reality. An analysis of language is interested in one reality: it is the accurate use of language to state the meaning of language. But if language can be used to express an interpretation of a reality other than language, it is dogmatic to insist that the only philosophical function of language is to clarify the meaning of language itself.

A language sign can be interpreted in language only by means of language. But after this has been acknowledged, nothing whatever has been said about anything which is other than language. Yet, the amazement for what can be said about a few symbols accounts for a sophisticated people having almost the primitive's awe for language. Most of the cause for this awe, however, in language analysis is fabricated by the analysis itself. As Bertrand Russell remarks, "The purely logical analysis of 'Dogs bark' soon reaches complexities which make it incredible that ordinary folk can seem to understand anything so remote (and) mysterious." (6)

An analysis of a statement may be complex, but the complex analysis does not increase the complexity of the statement analyzed. It is the analysis which is complex, but its complexity is not an index to the structure of the analyzed statement, or of the thought expressed in the simple statement. Anyone who has proficiency with a musical instrument, for example, is able to take a phrase of music and spin out variation after variation until well-nigh the infinite series itself of such operations seems to have transpired before the feat comes to a close. But no musically sensitive ear confuses this demonstration of endurance with musical creativity. A musician is a true artist not by his capacity to drive a simple phrase to death, but rather by his ability to create phrases with vitality, and integrate them into a composition. The vitality of music is the musical content; not the technique of expressing the same figure over and over again in so many ways that there are no more combinations possible within the limits of audible octaves. This exhibition of skill as a substitute for creativity, is, however, too often the genius of language analysis itself.

Just as "variations on a theme" may continue on and on until the range of musical enjoyment itself constricts to one pattern of sound, so an analysis of language may go on and on, until one believes that nothing else exists except the explication of one symbol in terms of other symbols.

As all skills, language analysis, Professor Whitehead has said, has "a tendency to run wild", so that people "can easily be overwhelmed by . . . symbolic accessories." (7) Individuals who develop skills are often tempted to over-use their skills, and as Ogden and Richards have declared, "The ablest logicians are precisely those who are led to evolve the most fantastic systems by the aid of their verbal techniques." (8)

But too often an operation upon a statement does not even clarify the meaning of the statement: it rather creates other statements more difficult to comprehend than the one which it sought to clarify.

There are indeed many statements which need no commentary. They already have a meaning clear to anyone who is able to use language well enough to propose another statement to explicate it. When such is the case, the office of language analysis is officious. But it is the same officious service which is too often performed by those having little which is significant to say, and yet having many words with which to say something. This is "the poverty of human understanding copious in words" of which St. Augustine speaks. (9)

Language may be used to state an interpretation of a reality other than language, and it may also be used to state an interpretation of the statement of the interpretation. To interpret a reality other than language, however, one must have some understanding of a reality other than language. Yet, even though one does not have such understanding, he may, nevertheless, have an aptitude to interpret language itself. A knowledge-claim to the nature of a reality other than language should, therefore, never be confused with a knowledge of language. Even if one were to know everything about language, he would know only the nature of one of the instruments which man has developed to express his interpretation.

2

AN ANALYSIS OF LANGUAGE AS A STUDY OF GRAMMAR

WHEREAS logic has often been regarded in the history of philosophy as a set of conditions essential for thinking, it is more and more regarded as a system of rules stipulating language uses. Instead of regarding the law of excluded middle, for example, as a necessary condition for thinking, it is looked upon as an agreement that whatever is not designated by one term, shall be designated by its negative. According to this modern point of view, the logical principle of excluded middle does not designate the manner in which it is necessary to think. It merely stipulates one of the ways in which it is possible to express thinking. Whatever, for example, is not classified as "white" must be classified as "non-white", but the necessity in this case is simply the necessity to conform to what one says.

Thus the "law of excluded middle" according to this point of view expresses an agreement about the use of a symbol to designate a single term of discourse, and the use of its negation to designate every other item of discourse.

But after this much has been said, it may also be said

that more than language conforms to this principle. Non-linguistic experience likewise conforms to the pattern of this principle. An individual, for example, either is on a train when it leaves a station, or he is not. Even if he used no language to express his dismay when coming to a station after a train had gone, he would, nevertheless, be confronted by the fact that he did not get on the train. One need not be a specialist in language to recognize that there is a mutual exclusiveness in experiences as well as in the senses of language symbols, and one need never use language, and still act in accordance with the principle of excluded middle. But one couldn't talk about any act without conforming to the principle as a "rule of language use".

Whatever is said, if it is intelligible, is stated in conformity to the principle of excluded middle as a rule of language. But an interpretation of experience, even if not stated in language, nevertheless, conforms to the same pattern. The very maxim of common sense, for example, that "one cannot have his cake and eat it too" is a lesson learned far below the level of linguistic aptitude. An experience is what it is by virtue of its otherness from all that it is not, and if anything is distinguishable in experience from everything else in experience, such distinction is an instance of the excluded middle.

What has been said about the excluded middle may also be said about the other two traditional "laws" or "principles": identity, and non-contradiction.

A symbol has language significance only when it designates an item in the realm of discourse which is distinguishable from other items. If no feature within experience could be distinguished from other features, there would be no occasion for language. In such a context, only the extreme mystic would be at home: everything would be an undifferentiated totality.

But thinking is distinguishing, and whatever is distinguishable has some identity. Yet, if more than symbols constitute the sum total of reality, then it is dogmatic to maintain that the principle of identity is *only* a prescription for the use of language. It is this; but it is also more than this.

The agreement to use a symbol in only one way would indeed be inconsistent with the practice of using it in another way. Such inconsistency indeed "is something which can be located only in discourse." (1) Yet, the same may not be said about the principle of excluded middle, and the principle of identity. If there is anything whose identity is its own property, then the principle of identity is not only a condition for the use of language: it is also an interpretation of a feature of a non-linguistic reality.

The analysis of language today has developed into a highly skilled autonomous science. As such, it has become a set of principles sufficient to stipulate all the operations which may be performed upon symbols internal to a symbolic system, and a complete analysis of the meaning of statements in a symbolic system is a set of logical inferences which constitute the full meaning of the statements. Thus the ideal of logical thinking is restating a proposition in as many ways as it is linguistically possible to do so, without affirming more than is already asserted in the original statement. To be strictly logical, therefore, one need not think about some non-linguistic reality: he need think consistently only about a statement.

No matter what a statement may affirm, it is possible to be consistent with it. Even if a statement is a trivial

16

tautology, it is, nevertheless, possible to restate it in many ways. The meaning of such restatements would, however, be no less trivial than the meaning of the original. Yet, trivial as such restatements may be, they nonetheless constitute a superior specimen of logical thinking. Hence an individual's thinking may be thoroughly logical if he knows nothing whatsoever other than the rules for restating what has already been stated, and if all restatements of statements are according to the rules of warranted inference, thinking is completely logical. In performing this logical feat, one does, as has been said, to perfection what any "automatic thinking-machine" (2) would do if set to perform a specific number of operations in a specific way without any deviation whatsoever.

Yet, such a machine would no more have a capacity to comment upon the utility of its invention than a "completely logical" individual would have to comment upon the truth-character of the proposition from which he thinks. One could be a master of logical thinking, and know nothing of science, of history, or of anything else; provided only he had the skill to think within the limits of a thought expressed in a statement. When, for example, the conjunctive "and" is used to affirm that two components in a statement must be thought together, a logical analysis of this connective becomes an exhaustive statement of all that may, and may not, be said if one is to remain in accord with the stated meaning. Since the statement affirms *both*, one may not then affirm that it is *either* one *or* the other. If one were to presume the option of one or the other of the affirmed components, he simply would not "know" the linguistic operation designated by a conjunctive. His linguistic activity would be "illogical". It would be illogical because it is grammatically incorrect to identify these two statements. The affirmation, for example, that "man must work *and* pray" means that both components of the statement must be taken together. When this is affirmed, it is also affirmed that one does not have the option "either to work or to pray".

A concern with the rules of language, by means of which one remains consistent with a given statement, exhausts the concern of logic. But when logic is construed to be a grammar of language, it is not concerned with the "truth-character" of a statement which interprets a non-language reality. The so-called "science of logic", therefore, is a systematic enumeration only of the operations which may be performed upon a statement of a certain form. The principles for forming the initial statement are rules of ordinary grammar, and the principles for operating upon the statement in order to remain consistent with it are rules of formal logic.

Thus formal logic is regarded in modern language analysis as a specialized interpretation of grammar, and the function of grammar is simply to facilitate language use. But if experiences were never interpreted in a language-form, there would be no occasion for grammar, and so no practical need for logic. The practical function of logic is to facilitate the use of language, but when the ideal of all language-use is logical analysis, the practical function of language is completely ignored, and the scope of philosophy itself becomes confined to a study of grammar. This, however, is not a method of language analysis: it is a dogmatic judgment upon the nature of what is philosophically significant for analysis, and such a presumption is entirely outside the warranted function of any method of language analysis. As a dogmatic philosophy, it passes judgment not upon itself as a method;

but rather upon itself as the content of philosophically significant thought.

1. *A contemporary point of view is that truth is a feature simply of language.*

A statement which expresses an interpretation of a reality other than discourse is, however, "true" by a criterion which is not within the scope of language analysis. The conditions which make a statement "true" by virtue of information of a non-language reality are not rules of language.

The term "truth", therefore, is used today in two entirely different senses, and in order to avoid ambiguity, some analysts of language have maintained that truth is a property of a statement determined by the rules of grammar alone; and not by virtue of an interpretation expressed as the meaning of a statement. When truth, however, is used in this sense as the *only* legitimate sense, dogmatism displaces analysis, and becomes itself a metaphysic. It presumes to know that there is no interpretation possible of any reality other than language itself. But this, of course, is to presume that one knows something about the nature of everything.

Truth is a property of a statement, but a statement has the property of truth only by virtue of the interpretation it expresses. If a statement articulates an interpretation of another statement, it is the linguistic reality which determines whether the interpretation is informed. If, however, the statement expresses an informed interpretation of a non-language reality, it is the nature of this other-than-language reality which determines the truth of the statement.

If truth is a property of a statement which expresses

an informed interpretation, then statements which are logically inferred from other statements may be said to be true, as well as statements which express interpretations of a reality which is other than language. "Truth" as a property of a statement which expresses an informed interpretation is thus inclusive enough to be applied to a purely formal system, such as logic or calculus; and also to a system which is not entirely formal, such as a physical science, or a theology.

The sense of truth as logical validity, therefore, differs in no respect from the sense of truth as a property of an informed statement in the physical sciences. As a property of a statement which expresses an informed interpretation, the term "truth" is applicable to an inference from another statement, as well as to a statement which is not an inference from another statement.

According to this use of the term "truth", it is not necessary to distinguish between truth as a property of a statement which follows according to the rules of a formal system, and the truth of a statement which interprets a non-language reality. If the statement of an interpretation of sensory data, for example, affirms features of sensory experience, so that in the statement one is informed of the experience, then the statement is true.

Truth as a property of a statement therefore is determined by the adequacy of an interpretation which is expressed in language. What is determined by rules of language is the formation of a statement which expresses an interpretation.

It would be impossible for anyone to understand a statement unless he were aware of the rules according to which terms are used. But after understanding the rules of a language, an individual is informed of something

20

other than the formation of a statement when he interprets a true statement. If a statement is true by the criterion of the adequacy of an interpretation it expresses, then it is capable of informing another, not only about the interpretation, but also about what is interpreted.

Language is one instrument for expressing an interpretation, but language is not the only reality which is known. Yet, when it is maintained that language is all that is known, it obviously follows that the only possible object of philosophical study must be language, and nothing else. When, therefore, this is maintained, the sense of "truth" is confined to a property of statements, determined exclusively by rules of sentence formation.

So far as it goes, this very widespread interpretation is sound, but it expresses only a part of an analysis of language-functions. Language is an instrument for expressing interpretations. Yet, interpretations in human life are not all confined to the way language terms are used. Interpretations of realities other than language are also expressed by means of language. Thus when it is maintained that language is the *only* object of which knowledge may be claimed, one merely expresses a preference to study language according to the rules of conventional language-use. Although this is certainly one object of possible study, it is, nevertheless, sheer dogmatism to maintain that language has no interpretative or "philosophical function" other than stating an analysis of language.

Yet, even this widespread contemporary dogmatism is nothing new in the history of philosophy. It is as old as the Academy. Aristotle criticized the Academy for its preoccupation with a study of language, as if language itself were the only reality to be philosophically interpreted. He declared that "mathematics has been turned by our present day thinkers into the whole of philosophy, in spite of their declaration that it ought to be studied for the sake of something further." (3) This, however, is not a criticism of Plato: it is a criticism of those who with less to say than Plato, confine themselves entirely to a study of language. Yet, this is a phenomenon common within philosophy: when men have no interpretation to articulate either of life, or of the world in which they live, they turn upon language itself.

Salutary as a study of language may be, it is also a symptom: it is a symptom that the wells of vitality in philosophy are drying up, even though the skills for a manipulation of language are not. Yet, when skills persist, although insight does not, philosophy, as well as the rest of human life, spiritually perishes.

Plato, fortunately, did not limit his philosophy to an analysis of language. He believed that, important as a knowledge of language is, there are other objects which can be known which are even more significant in man's life than a knowledge of all conceivable linguistic minutiae. An ability to use language is, according to Plato, simply one condition for philosophy: it is not, however, equivalent to all philosophy. Plato endeavoured to express in language his interpretations of human life and the world in which man lives; and an interpretation of these other-than-language realities is for him the objective of philosophical analysis. Hence, he declares that knowledge of language is merely a "prelude to the hymn which has to be learned". (4)

When anyone has a point of view to express, he must, of course, first learn the language with which he proposes to express his point of view. But if he maintains that all of his beliefs are confined to an information about the rules of language itself, he merely designates that the exclusive object of his interest is grammar. To presume, however, that one declares something about the limits of language when he merely expresses his preference for study is pure dogmatism.

Yet, one of the common expressions of this very dogmatism is the position that the only differences in philosophies are differences in statements. This current point of view is the philosophy of Conventionalism. It affirms that nothing should be claimed as knowledge in science, religion, or philosophy except language-uses or conventions.

Language is indeed a convention. But certain linguistic conventions have evolved to express interpretations of realities other than language. Yet, when it is maintained as a philosophical dogma that only language-conventions can be known, it is obvious that the scope of all possible knowledge, and all warranted knowledge-claims, is delimited to an analysis of language-forms.

When, however, it is maintained that the *only* object which can be known is language, one is not analyzing language. He is affirming a dogmatic knowledge-claim known as Nominalism. The point of view of the "New Nominalism" is that the designative function of language is exhausted within language itself: that is, "designation" is a purely formal term. The argument of the New Nominalists is that the significance of every language-term is exhausted in the medium of language itself. Hence, even the term "designate" has only a linguistic significance, and does not indicate a reference to a reality beyond language.

This certainly is pressing a point as far as consistency

can go. But the price of this consistency is the use of language to deny that there is any other function for language to perform except to speak about itself. Such preoccupation with itself is not, however, the function which language performs outside of philosophical analysis; and important as analysis is, it is after all only one aspect of human experience, and it expresses only one use of language.

When the term "designation" is limited to a purely formal function, as it is in the New Nominalism, all statements are true or false "in a purely formal sense". This means that the only criterion by which their truth-character can be assessed is rules of language-use.

That the rules of language must be appealed to in order to pass judgment upon a use of language, no one would deny. What may, however, be denied is that a statement formed according to language rules is meaningful only by the criterion of grammar. If every statement can be "decidable on purely formal grounds" (5) then there is no experience which has scientific, or philosophical, or religious significance other than linguistic experience itself. To maintain this, however, is certainly dogmatic.

2. *Another contemporary point of view is that empirical sciences are simply instances of formal deduction.*

One very widespread tendency in the modern interpretation of language is to consider pure mathematics as the norm of all language-uses. Hence the conditions which prescribe the formation of a mathematical system are looked upon as the sufficient conditions for prescribing all language-uses in the sciences. But a mathematical system, such as calculus, however, does not provide an exhaustive analysis of the nature of language. It provides only an analysis of one specialized use of language. Hence, when mathematics is regarded as the "ideal" of language-use, the very norm of language-use becomes a false clue for the analysis of language in the physical sciences.

A mathematical system is an internally consistent set of deductions from statements which are "given". These "given" statements stipulate the scope within which thinking must be confined, and a complete analysis of them is the ideal of mathematics as a formal system. But physical science does not consist only of an interpretation of symbols: it uses symbols to express interpretations of non-symbolic reality. Symbols are known, but in so far as they designate interpretations of a reality which is other than symbols, the symbols are not the only objects which are known. The interpretations also are known, and if these interpretations are informed of the nature of the non-symbolic reality, then the symbolic statements are true.

An interpretation of a non-symbolic reality as a point of view may be stated symbolically. But the point of view is not an arbitrary language convention. Language symbols with a sense, which is determined by convention, are used to express a point of view which is not always determined by convention.

Thus, two entirely different types of knowledge are presupposed in stating points of view in science. One is a knowledge of the sense of symbols. The other is a knowledge of an interpretation which one proposes to express by means of symbols.

Symbols in physical science, for example, are selected

RELIGIOUS FAITH, LANGUAGE, AND KNOWLEDGE

on the basis of the correspondence of their sense to the interpretation of a non-symbolic reality. This, however, is not the rule of procedure in any strictly formal system, as mathematics. A formal system is the deductive elaboration of a set of postulates, and the postulates specify what may be thought within the system. If the postulates state a significant addition to knowledge, a deductive analysis of them adds to knowledge. But if the postulates are trivial, a deductive elaboration of them is no less trivial.

When the ideal of language, therefore, is a formal deductive system, the ideal of language even in physical sciences then becomes statements which assert interpretation only of language-uses. The advances, however, which have been made in the history of science are manifestations of the fruitfulness of interpretations of a reality other than language. Logical consistency within a deductive system cannot account for the technological achievements resulting from scientific research. Research in the physical sciences is an operation upon the structures of non-symbolic realities in order to interpret them in terms of symbols. But after interpretations have been formulated, what is stated is not the conventional sense of symbols: rather, symbols with sense are selected to express interpretations of realities other than symbols.

The ideal of a purely formal discipline, therefore, cannot be proposed as the ideal for an interpretation of a reality other than language. It is not an ideal for religious interpretations of the divine reality any more than it is an ideal for a scientific interpretation of a physical reality. Neither a divine reality, which religious faith endeavors to interpret, nor a physical reality, whose structure physical science endeavours to understand, are language symbols. They are realities other than the symbols with which interpretations are symbolically expressed.

If there were nothing more to interpret than the total senses which have been associated with certain symbols, obviously an exhaustive enumeration of these senses would constitute all that could be known. If the reality of God, for example, were as George Santayana affirms, nothing more than a "floating literary symbol" with which any sense may be associated, then an enumeration of these senses would be an exhaustive analysis of the complete nature of God. But this interpretation of the reality of God is merely an instance of the dogmatic metaphysic that the only reality to which religious faith can be directed is itself a product of faith.

For such a dogmatic subjectivism, an analysis of symbols as conventions is an analysis of their knowledge-value. But a language-symbol is simply a designation for a sense, and the sense is not the symbol. The sense of the symbol is what the symbol designates.

When, however, a purely formal system, such as symbolic logic, or calculus, is looked upon as the norm of all language use, language itself is analyzed in accommodation to a dogmatic philosophy of language. Hence, when the meaning of statements is said to be the only object of which knowledge may be claimed, one does not merely state a philosophy of language. He also states a theory of knowledge.

To confine warranted knowledge-claims, however, to an analysis of language "presupposes", as Kant has pointed out, "neither greater reflexion nor deeper insight than to detect in a language the rules of the actual use of words generally, and thus to collect elements for a grammar." (6)

But this is not a philosophy of language: it is also a dogmatic theory of knowledge. It proposes the type of reality to which knowledge-claims must be limited.

3

A PHILOSOPHY OF LANGUAGE ANALYSIS AS A THEORY OF SCIENTIFIC KNOWLEDGE

EVERY analysis of language begins with some assumptions about the functions of language. When these assumptions state what can be known when language is used, they constitute a theory of knowledge.

The transition from a theory of language to a theory of knowledge is thus easy. The very ease with which this transition occurs accounts for the fact that when a method of language analysis is stated as a philosophy of language, it becomes a philosophy of knowledge.

A philosophy of language is not merely an analysis of what is affirmed in language: it is rather a statement of what may be the affirmed in language. This difference is very great. It is the difference between a method of acquiring information about what is stated, and a theory about what is known when one understands a statement.

A statement may be analyzed in order to clarify its meaning. When this is done, the statement itself becomes an object of knowledge. But if such an analysis is the only philosophically warranted knowledge, obviously nothing more may be claimed as knowledge than the meaning of statements. Such an analysis is an operation upon language, and according to contemporary Logical Empiricism, knowledge is confined to an analysis of language expressions. When every statement, therefore, which may be inferred from a given statement is known, one has exhausted the range of warranted knowledge-claims.

As was pointed out in the last chapter, Kant declared that a complete knowledge of the forms of statements "presupposes neither greater reflexion nor deeper insight than to detect in a language the rules for the actual use of words." (1) This could be said by any logical empiricist, although Kant is not a logical empiricist. According to Kant, the forms of statements do not have their origin in experience. The logical empiricists, on the other hand, maintain that they do.

Kant maintains that when we exhaustively know the structure of our statements, we know the structure of the human "mind". He argues that although our statements may vary according to the peculiarities of particular experiences, there is no variability in the basic forms of statements which can be affirmed: these forms are constant, and an analysis of them constitutes the only "universally valid" knowledge which may philosophically be defended.

1. *Kant's analysis of language-forms is a theory of scientific knowledge.*

What we know, according to Kant, are the forms in which all claims to knowledge are asserted. These are the forms of "our cognition", and they inform us of the nature of "the cognitive faculty". (2) In knowing these, we may not therefore assume that we are informed of anything external to them. That there is some reality external to our organized experiences, Kant does not doubt; he merely denies the warrant to claim any knowledge of it.

2. *Kant does not discredit the realistic hypothesis*: *he affirms the dualistic theory of knowledge.*

Experiences, according to Kant, do not "represent things as they are in themselves" (3), and so the "peculiar way in which we think . . . must be clearly distinguished from an insight into the objects themselves." (4)

This distinction, however, which Kant makes is unwarranted on empiricist grounds. It is pure dogmatism to maintain that *none* of our experiences offer "an insight into the objects" as they exist apart from our sensibility. This denial is, in fact, merely a logical deduction from the presupposition of the duality of objects as organized experiences, and as objects existing apart from experience. What Kant infers from his presupposition is logically sound, but the warrant for his dualistic presupposition is a different matter: and it is not a matter of logic.

That there is something other than organized experience, and other than the *a priori* conditions for organizing experience, Kant does not deny. He denies only that we can know anything of any reality which exists external to experience. But this cannot be known on empirical grounds. We know the forms of our statements by analyzing our statements. But there is no basis whatever, either in logic or in a theory of knowledge, to maintain as dogmatically as Kant does, that in knowing such forms we know *nothing* of any realities existing apart from them.

It is sheer dogmatism, for example, to maintain that the spatial pattern in which experiences are organized "is not at all a quality of things." (5) That there may be no acquaintance in experience with the structure of a reality existing apart from experience is possible; but that there is no such acquaintance, is something which we cannot know.

The dogmatic position of Kant is two-edged. By the same point of view according to which he affirms that we cannot know that our experiences inform us of anything existing apart from experience, he must also admit that we cannot know that they do not so inform us. If, however, there are realities existing apart from experience, as Kant assumes there are, it is theoretically possible that something of their nature may be known in our experience. But Kant denies this. Yet, one may have such acquaintance even though he cannot know that he has, and cannot verify that he has. Kant, of course, is unable to "verify" that there isn't such acquaintance, just as anyone is unable to verify that there is.

The only basis for Kant's denial of all knowledge of a reality transcendent of experience is his dogmatic dualistic presupposition. Yet, it is this very presupposition which must be challenged on grounds of critical empiricism itself. On empirical grounds, it is unwarranted to maintain that "intuitions . . . never concern any other things than objects of our senses." (6) The only grounds for defending such a claim is logical consistency. *If* "objects of experiences are themselves experiences; and *if* all we can know are our experiences, we indeed know only "objects of experience".

But this delimitation of knowledge to such objects is a definition of knowledge in terms of "experience". Knowledge, however, may be defined differently; it may be defined as an acquaintance with the nature of realities by means of experience. According to this definition, what is known are also "objects of experience", but the meaning of the phrase "objects of experience" differs from Kant's meaning.

Yet, more than one point of view is possible in defining the nature of knowledge, because more than one definition of "objects of knowledge" is possible. In so far as Kant is an empiricist, he may maintain that "experience . . . contain (s) all the objects of our concepts", although from this presupposition it does not follow that "beyond it no concepts have any significance." (7) We know our experience, but we do not know that our experience informs us of nothing other than experience.

3. *Kant's theory of knowledge is a dogmatism.*

Kant's denial of all knowledge of reality transcendent of experience does not follow from empiricist assumptions: it follows only from a dogmatic premise that beyond experiences, and their organizing forms, nothing is known. The denial of such knowledge, however, is an independent presupposition. It is that "nothing whatever can be thought by (the categories) beyond the field of experience." (8)

It is, nevertheless, possible that there are objects existing external to our experiences, something of whose nature we are informed of in our experiences. This assumption, however, cannot be verified by experience, since this would appeal to experience to verify a statement about a nature which is other than experience. But because it cannot be verified, Kant concludes it must be denied. It is this denial, however, which is unwarranted on the grounds of Kant's empiricism; and because another position is possible, which is also consistent with empiricism, Kant's position is dogmatic.

Kant maintains, for example, that the concept is *our* concept. This is obvious; but what is not equally obvious is that because it is our concept, it "necessarily belongs to the *mere* form of experience". (9) That it may be a feature only of experience cannot be denied on the grounds of consistent empiricism, and, on the same grounds, it cannot be affirmed. But according to Kant, number concepts do not inform us of anything beyond experience: "the unity of the objects is entirely determined by the understanding." (10) Yet, the insistence of Kant upon the "entire" determination is dogmatic. Even though number concepts are "determined by understanding", there is no way to know that a reality external to understanding does not also have a character which is interpreted by our number concepts. It is possible that there is an ordered reality existing external to our experience which is interpreted by our conceptual order. Kant, however, denies this possibility by the affirmation that whatever "laws of nature" we know are *only* the laws which inhere in our understanding. (11) But it is possible that in knowing the structure of our experiences, we also know something of a reality which makes an impact upon our capacities for experience. Although Kant assumes such a relation to a reality external to experience, he, nevertheless, dogmatically denies its knowledge significance.

Although one must say that *our experiences* are our experiences, it does not follow that there is no correlation between features of experience and features of a reality external to experience. *Claims to knowledge* are experiences, and there are no knowledge-claims which are other than experiences. In this sense, Kant is certainly warranted in saying that there is no "knowledge lying beyond experience." (12) But he may well be challenged for his dogmatism in saying that there is no possibility of having knowledge of any reality "lying beyond experience."

4. *Kant assumes as warranted a dogmatic rationalistic point of view in his empirical analysis.*

Kant was not satisfied with Hume's analysis as the last word in a theory of knowledge of science because implied in his analysis is a denial of science, as Kant tent" of empirical statements, he believed, as Hume did that particular sensory experiences constitute the "content" of empirical statements, he believed, as Hume did not, that a universal statement about sensory experiences is warranted. It is this warrant which he defends by assuming that there are forms with which particular sensory experiences are organized. These forms, he maintains, are *a priori* in the sense that they are not derived from experience: they are "necessary" conditions for it, and as such, precede *all* experiences.

As an empiricist, however, Kant assumes that these forms can be discovered only by an analysis of organized experiences. Although this is an empiricist's point of view, it is a non-empiricist's dogmatism to maintain that the forms discovered by analyzing experiences are the only possible forms for organizing experiences. Kant, for example, assumes that the categories of Euclidean geometry are the only possible concepts in a geometrical system. It is, however, a fact that we are learning to think in terms of non-Euclidean geometries, and thus are learning that the possible forms for our thinking are not so absolute as Kant assumed they are.

Kant declares that one may "refute" his position only "by producing a single synthetical proposition . . . which he could *prove* dogmatically *a priori.*" (13) This, of course, is impossible: it is impossible to "prove" in experience a statement about the nature of something other than experience. Yet, although this assumption cannot be "proved" in the sense of being empirically "verified", it does not, by any means, follow that there may be no knowledge of a reality external to experience. We *may* assume that some of our experiences acquaint us with the nature of realities which are other than our experiences, although we cannot verify this assumption.

The assumption, however, that there *may* be such a knowledge is not even congenial to Kant's dogmatism. As a dogmatic rationalist, who tried also to be an empiricist, Kant rejects the notion of probable knowledge as the basis for science or metaphysics, declaring that "nothing can be more absurd than . . . to think of grounding our judgments upon probability and conjecture." (14)

There is, however, more than one interpretation of science and metaphysics. If both are conceived as systems of statements about a reality existing external to the statements themselves, it may be assumed that some of the statements express an interpretation of it. There is no way to demonstrate that they do; but one may have knowledge defined as true beliefs, and yet not be able to demonstrate that he has such knowledge.

Kant defines a reality external to experience in such a way that it is contradictory to affirm any knowledge-claim of it. He defines it as a "thing in itself" whose nature cannot be known in experience. Obviously it follows from the definition itself that "reason does not . . . teach us anything concerning" it. (15) When Kant, therefore, speaks of "the object we know", he means "objects of the senses". But, it is trivial to point out, as he does, that "to give them a self-subsisting existence apart from experience . . . is merely to represent to ourselves that experience actually exists apart from experience." (16) It is obvious that objects which are organized experiences do not exist "apart from experience", and to maintain that they do would be a contradiction. Yet, it is not a contradiction to maintain that there may be objects existing apart from our experiences whose nature to some extent may be known in our experiences.

Since this is an assumption, it cannot be "proved"; and to propose "proof" for such an assumption would be unworthy of anyone who understands the nature of a postulate. Kant, therefore, creates a straw man, which he defeats without difficulty, when he argues that it would be "contradictory to say that a mere mode of representation exists without our representation." (17) Surely no one who could understand the meaning of a statement would deny this. We do know our interpretations, and by an analysis of them we can ascertain the basic forms of our interpretations. By such an analysis, Kant argues that we have knowledge of the "principles" of our thinking. Although this claim to knowledge is consistent empiricism, it is nevertheless inconsistent with the nature of empiricism to affirm, as Kant does, that when we know this much, "nothing more . . . can be cognized in experience." (18)

There is no way to verify this hypothesis; but there is no way to verify any other hypothesis interpreting experience. An empiricist's hypothesis is a point of view according to which one interprets experience, and experience obviously cannot be cited as evidence to verify statements of the existence of something other than experience. *If,* however, something other than experience exists, and *if* we are related to it through our experiences, then it may be assumed that something of its nature conditions our point of view to the extent that our point of view may be informed of its nature.

Kant, however, discredits this hypothesis; but he does so only on the basis of his dogmatic denial of a knowledge of any reality existing external to experiences. Sensory experiences certainly do not provide evidence to substantiate Kant's position, because his position is a point of view with which sensory experiences are interpreted. That experience "in no respect" (19) enables us to be exists, and *if* we are related to it through our experience is merely the reaffirmation of a dogmatic definition of what is *not* known. Kant's dogmatic denial that our experience informs us of anything other than experience, and its organizing forms, is the premise itself with which he interprets experience. He confines the informative value of experience to experience, and denies it beyond experience: or as he himself declares, the "undoubted value" of experience is confined "only to experience." (20)

It is, however, the dogmatic character of Kant's affirmation of what *cannot* be known which constitutes the weakest link in the chain of his argument. What he declares we know about our experience may well be defended on empiricist grounds; but what he declares we do *not* know, cannot be defended on any grounds other than consistency with his dogmatic dualistic presupposition. One may well follow him in his "analytic", admitting that his interpretation of the forms in which we think is one possible interpretation, and yet one need not follow him in his dogmatic insistence that when this much is known, nothing more can be known.

5. *Kant maintains, as contemporary Positivism and Logical Empiricism maintain, that scientific knowledge is of statements and statement-forms.*

Kant did not assume, as contemporary empiricists in language analysis do assume, that statements are all that we can know. He believed that there are sensory data (*Anschauung*) which we interpret. Although indebted to the radical empiricist Hume for pointing out to him the necessity to take sensory data into account in analyzing the nature of knowledge-claims, he did not follow Hume's radical empiricism.

Hume, of course, was not a scientist, and Kant was. Kant, therefore, was concerned as a philosopher to defend the warrant for making universal judgments, and Kant construed universality to mean "necessity" in the sense that propositions in science express what must be thought; not merely what is thought.

This was not Hume's concern; and Kant himself points out this difference when he says that Hume's problem was a question concerning the origin, not concerning the indispensable need of a concept. (21) According to Hume, as an empiricist, "necessity . . . is nothing but a long habit of accepting something as true," (22) and so according to him, "causation arises entirely from the uniformity observable . . . where similar objects are constantly conjoined, and the mind is determined by custom to infer the one from the appearance of the other." (23)

This is indeed an analysis of the origin of the idea of causation. But this analysis of the idea of what is causally connected does not account for the sequence of experiences whose regularity constitutes the very motive in an analysis of experience for proposing an explanatory principle which is other than experience. Hume does not propose to explain this, and therefore acknowledges "what that medium is, I must confess, passes my comprehension." (24) The attempt, however, to account for it gave rise to Kant's analysis.

A strictly empirical analysis cannot account for anything other than features of experiences. Hence, Hume says that when he uses the term "custom", he does not propose to give "the ultimate reason of such a propensity." He merely designates the way experiences are organized: or as he says, "we only point out a principle of human nature." (25)

Yet, there is enough ambiguity in Hume's statement to say that Kant's analysis begins with the same proposition. Kant is also concerned to analyze the "principle of human nature" as expressed in statements claiming scientific knowledge.

Contemporary Logical Empiricism also attempts to analyze the nature of knowledge, but it does not follow the radical empiricism of Hume so much as it follows the rationalistic dogmatism of Kant. It maintains, as Kant does, that the *only* objects of "scientific knowledge" are "forms of statements", and it also maintains, as Kant does, that the forms of warranted statements constitute the *only* science which can be known, which is a "logic of science".

6. *Logical Empiricism as a theory of scientific knowledge is Positivism.*

When one maintains, however, that knowledge in science is limited to the "logic of science" (*Wissenschafts-logik*), one defends Positivism. Positivism is a theory that knowledge in science is confined to "statements about the physical". Yet, this statement could not be more ambiguous, and its ambiguity is well illustrated in a recent book by Sir James Jeans, entitled *Physics and Philosophy*. (26)

Jeans maintains that "physics tries to discover the pattern of events which controls the phenomena we observe." (27) From this assertion it appears as if he were maintaining that the object of which scientific knowledge is claimed is the physical world. It is this realistic hypothesis which seems to be assumed when he declares that statements in physics "import real knowledge into our minds" in formulae which express "the value of a ratio which has an existence in the world outside." (28) The realistic hypothesis seems also to be affirmed in the statements that "the method of science" is the "one possible source of knowledge as to the special properties of our own world" (29), and "the only sound method is to go into the world and question nature directly . . . to discover the truth about nature." (30)

What, however, is actually affirmed is that scientific knowledge is confined to metrical statements: not to the physical world whose properties are expressed in measurements, and this meaning becomes explicit in the assertion that "the values of ratios . . . constitute the raw

41

material of physics." (31) The only possible knowledge, therefore, which we may claim in science, according to Jeans, is a knowledge of our experiences, and this position is clearly affirmed when he asserts that "there is no compelling reason why phenomena—the mental visions that a mind constructs out of electric currents in a brain —should resemble the objects that produced these currents in the first instance." (32) The possibility of knowing anything of a reality external to experience itself is, furthermore, clearly denied by the statement that "the messages we receive . . . through the windows of our senses . . . tell us nothing as to the essential nature of their origins." (33) Jeans, therefore, maintains that "we can never understand what events are, but must limit ourselves to describing the pattern of events in mathematical terms." (34)

The "pattern of events" of which he speaks, however, is ambiguous. One assumes that it is the pattern of events in the physical world which we measure, and which we express in our scientific formulae. But this is not the meaning intended by Jeans, and this fact becomes clear when he says that "the study of physics has driven us to the positivist conception". (35) This means one thing. Knowledge is not of the physical world: it is of measurements, and measurements which are expressed as statements. Such statements, according to Positivism, are not "of something": this is the very knowledge-claim which Positivism historically has always repudiated. What is known, according to historical Positivism, and according to Jeans' theory of scientific knowledge, are statements of metrical symbols.

The pivotal problem which is at stake in criticizing contemporary positivism, and Jeans' positivistic theory in particular, is not whether we can know everything of the physical world. It is whether we can know anything. Jeans and contemporary Positivists, however, confuse mathematics as a means for expressing knowledge-claims of a physical world with mathematics as the only object of which there is knowledge in science. Yet, mathematics may be both an instrument for expressing knowledge-claims, and also an object of knowledge. When it is an instrument for expressing claims to a knowledge of the physical world, it refers beyond itself to interpretations of the metrical character of a reality which is other than the mathematical expressions.

The problem, therefore, is whether we have knowledge only of our experience, or whether we have knowledge of something other than experience, and by means of experience. It is trivial to observe, as Jeans does, that our ideas which are expressed in science are subjective. Yet, what is not trivial, but absolutely fundamental to any philosophy of knowledge is the decision whether ideas, which are subjective, have an objective reference, so that they interpret a reality whose nature validates them as informed, and so as true ideas.

The basic problem, therefore, in a theory of scientific knowledge is the criterion by which the truth-character of statements in science is to be judged. The problem is whether statements in physical science are true because internally consistent, as in mathematical systems; or, if they are also true as linguistic expressions of interpretations of a reality external to, and other than, the statements themselves.

It is trite to say, as Jeans does, that "it is useless to try to understand the workings of nature except in terms of ideas." (36) One must ask, "What other means could there be for understanding?" The real problem is whether in knowledge-claims we are confined to our ideas, or whether our ideas are capable of interpreting the character of a world external to our ideas. This is not asking if reality is rational, as rationalistic philosophies have argued. It is only asking if our ideas, in however partial a manner, constitute information of something other than ideas.

In spite of the particular failure of Jeans to state a consistent positivistic position, a consistent statement of the positivistic position is, nevertheless, possible, and it has been accomplished by the so-called Viennese Circle of Positivists (*Wiener Kreis*). These philosophers maintain that knowledge-claims must be confined within experience, and since the experiences which constitute the content of knowledge-claims in science are statements, they maintain that what is known in science are statements.

When this position, however, is pressed for a clarification of what is expressed in a statement in physical science, it actually becomes many diverse points of view. Thus when the method of language analysis is applied to the very philosophy which makes the most of the program of language analysis, the greatest possible divergence occurs in clarifying the meaning of the term "knowledge" itself. The reason for this is clear: a clarification of the meaning of the term "knowledge" leads beyond an analysis of language.

The projected program of the Viennese Positivists is a "philosophical or logical analysis", which is construed by them to be "a clarification of the meaning of language." As a statement, this is intelligible, because grammatically correct. But just what the "meaning of meaning" is remains even for them an unresolved philosophical problem. If the meaning of a statement were to be exhausted in other statements, then an analysis of a statement would be a self-contained, thoroughly autonomous philosophy, and the sole criterion of knowledge would then be internal consistency.

But, if a system of language statements is the only object of knowledge, there would be no fundamental difference in a physical science and in formal systems, such as symbolic logic.

If, however, the statements in a physical science express an interpretation of a reality other than language, then the meaning of the statements can be clarified only by pointing to what they interpret. *If* language in physical science refers beyond itself, then language is *not* the only object of which knowledge is claimed in physical science, and if this referential function of language is acknowledged, one cannot be a consistent positivist.

The meaning of a statement as a language structure is one thing, and the meaning of a statement as an interpretation of a physical reality is another thing. When a statement expresses an interpretation of a reality other than language, the full meaning of the statement cannot be exhausted by other statements. There must, consequently, come a time in clarifying the meaning of such statements when one points to a reality other than statements.

4

AN EMPIRICAL ANALYSIS AS A PHILOSOPHY OF RELIGION

ONE of the best known books in the philosophy of religion written during this century is Rudolf Otto's *The Idea of the Holy*.

According to Otto, a religious individual knows experience: not a divine reality transcendent of experience. According to this neo-Kantian positivism, nothing can be known of a reality external to experience. Thus, what is interpreted by Otto as the "holy", or "the numinous", is not a divine reality: it is a type of experience. It is a type of experience which cannot be interpreted in terms of other experiences, and so it cannot be interpreted by the means of concepts.

The "holy" is not an attribute of God: it is an attribute of experience. It is a "mental state" which "cannot be strictly defined" because it is non-rational, and it is non-rational in the sense that it cannot be interpreted in concepts. When an attempt is made to interpret it, it becomes "conceptualized", or "rationalized". As a "numinous state of mind" (1), it is a "fact of *our* nature —primary, unique, underivable from anything else",

46

and is "the basic factor and the basic impulse underlying the entire process of religious evolution." (2)

Whatever, therefore, Otto says about the numinous is a psychological analysis of human experience: it is not an interpretation of a reality transcendent of experience. Otto believes, as Kant does, that every knowledge-claim must be confined to interpreted experience. Since no reality external to experience can be known in experience, or by means of experience, the numinous, or holy, is an "experience . . . belonging to the spirit of man." (3) It is not a feature of a divine reality. Experience itself confers religious significance upon human life: it is not a knowledge of a divine reality transcendent of human life which confers religious significance upon it.

Although Otto's analysis is consistent with Kant's theory of knowledge, it has, however, nothing whatsoever to do with interpreting religious experience as an individual with religious faith would interpret it.

According to Otto, the unique feature of religious life is not faith in a reality which is worthy of man's trust. Such a faith would affirm that there is a reality transcendent of human experience to which an individual turns because he believes it to be worthy of his trust. Such a faith, however, would not be warranted within the limits of Kant's theory of knowledge, since what alone can be known, according to Kant, is experience, and the forms according to which it is organized and interpreted.

Otto begins his analysis of religious life with this Kantian point of view, and then declares that "the most noteworthy phenomenon in the whole history of religion (is) the numinous consciousness" itself. (4) What alone is known in religious life, according to Otto, therefore is "the numinous consciousness" which emerges in due

47

course in the developing life of human mind and spirit and is thenceforward simply present. (5) He declares that this experience itself "humbles and at the same time exalts us." (6) Yet, no religious individual believes that experience is the reality which "humbles and at the same time exalts us." Religious faith is the conviction that one ought to be humbled before the One Reality upon which he acknowledges his complete dependence.

But again, Otto could not say this, since he interprets religious life from the point of view of a positivistic theory of knowledge, according to which warranted knowledge-claims are confined to experience. This certainly is not the religious individual's interpretation of religious experience. It is the point of view of a Kantian philosopher; and a Kantian interpreter of religious faith could be nothing more than a psychologist of religious experience. This is exactly what Otto is. His Kantian presuppositions make him reject the possibility of any knowledge of a reality transcendent of experience. Hence, whatever he says about religious experience is about experience itself: it is not about a reality transcendent of human life of which man has experience.

Otto's analysis of religious experience may be good psychology, but when it is proposed as the point of view of a religious individual, it is untenable. For example, Otto interprets Isaiah's affirmation "I am a man of unclean lips" to mean that Isaiah encountered "the numinous reality . . . as a present fact of consciousness." (7) "Fact of consciousness", however, has enough ambiguity to conceal exactly what Otto means. Yet, there is no ambiguity in what he means when he affirms that it is "this self-depreciating feeling-response" which "breaks

. . . like a direct reflex movement at the stimulation of the numinous." (8) According to this analysis, what Isaiah is confronted with is not a reality "high and lifted up"; it is with his own experience, and this is all that anyone can know according to a positivistic theory of knowledge which follows from a radical dualism such as Kant maintained.

Otto declares that "the feeling of one's own abasement, of being but 'dust and ashes' . . . forms the numinous raw material for the feeling of religious humility." (9) But this is a psychology of religious experience. It points out how an individual's feeling of his own "nothingness" is one ingredient in the numinous experience. This psychological analysis, however, does not account for self-abasement as a religious response to what a religious individual acknowledges as the "high and lifted up." Otto points out how one experience conditions another experience, which is obvious; but his analysis is not a statement of a religious individual's interpretation of religious experience. Such an interpretation affirms that man has a religious experience in relation to a reality before which he recognizes himself to be but dust and ashes.

1. *Language in religious interpretations, according to Otto, designates experience.*

The term "numinous" in Otto's analysis, as well as the terms "holy", and "mysterium", designate experience. What is holy and mysterious for a religious individual, according to Otto, is his own experience; "the profound element of *wonderfulness* and rapture . . . lies in the mysterious beatific experience." (10) This is a non-ambiguous way to state an analysis of experience in a way which is consistent with a Kantian theory of knowledge. But then it is unwarranted for Otto also to say that wonder in religious life "lies in the mysterious beatific experience of deity." (11)

The term "wholly other" likewise designates experience: the numinous experience is "wholly other" every other experience. As such it is non-translatable by any concept or interpretation. Hence it is a "primal feeling", and as such it is "unique". As a "unique . . . reality and quality", it is "something of whose special character we can *feel,* without being able to give it clear conceptual expression." (12) If, however, it were interpreted, and the interpretation stated in language terms, the feeling would be translated into what is not unique. Interpretations are concepts, and concepts which are designated by language terms are not "unique": they are intelligible to all who understand the language in which these terms are used.

Religious faith may be psychologically analyzed, but in so far as religious faith is a response to a reality which is other than experience, a psychology does not have the last word in an analysis of faith. A psychology of religious experience, therefore, should not be confused with a religious interpretation of a reality of which a religious individual believes he has experience. Although religious faith *as an experience* may be interpreted psychologically, the reality in which a religious individual believes he has faith cannot be interpreted psychologically. To maintain that it can, is sheer dogmatism.

According to religious faith, there is a reality in which an individual has faith; which reality justifies his faith; and so constitutes the warrant for his confidence in it and for his conviction of his dependence upon it. It is this conviction, however, which goes beyond the scope of psychology because it affirms a metaphysical presupposition. It affirms the belief that transcendent of experience is a divine reality which alone is completely trustworthy, and therefore is alone completely worthy to be trusted.

Yet, according to the Kantian theory of knowledge, any metaphysical statement about a reality transcendent of experience is unwarranted. Consistent, therefore, with this Kantian dogmatism, Otto maintains that language terms do not designate qualities of a reality existing apart from experience. Words which are ordinarily assumed to designate a property of a divine reality actually designate qualities of experience. "Wrath", for example in Otto's analysis, does not designate a feature of God's nature: it designates rather "a unique emotional moment in religious experience", which experience is "singularly daunting and awe-inspiring." (13)

Otto thus maintains the same position which Dionysius did: "the names of God. . . . are not descriptive of His own nature. Rather, they describe corresponding qualities in us." (14) Otto, furthermore, explicitly points out his agreement with Chrysostom's analysis of religious experience when he declares that the "incomprehensible is. . . . an intimate and essential possession of the human soul." (15)

Otto also speaks of "om" as a "holy syllable", and characterizes it as "an articulated sound" which is not even a "complete syllable". "It is simply a sort of growl or groan, sounding up from within as the quasi-reflex expression of profound emotion . . . and serving to relieve consciousness of a felt burden." (16) This is so obviously a psychological analysis of experience that no one could be mistaken about what he is speaking. Yet, its obvious character enables one to see just what Otto is speaking about in his entire analysis.

The Idea of the Holy, notwithstanding its widespread use as a theological study, is nothing more than a psychology of one type of experience. What is claimed to be known in this analysis, according to Otto, is not something about the nature of reality in which there is faith: it is a type of experience alone which is known.

Hence, according to Otto, it is possible for an individual to be religious without having any belief whatsoever about a divine reality to which he relates himself. Otto specifically says, "There is no need . . . for the experient to pass on to resolve his mere impression of the eerie and aweful into the idea of a 'numen', a divine power, . . . still less need the *numen* become a *nomen,* a named power." (17)

The untenability of Otto's analysis consequently becomes apparent when he maintains that it is possible for religious life to be without faith in a divine reality, and he cites, for example, the "German expression *es spukt hier* (literally, it haunts here)" as instructive of the nature of one instance of religious experience. Yet, the attempt to analyze any religious experience as an uninterpreted feeling is not an analysis of any religious experience: it is simply an abstraction. This abstraction is consistent with a Kantian theory of knowledge, but it reveals Otto's unwillingness to accept religious faith as a point of view which is warranted in interpreting one reality into relationship with which an individual may enter in his experience.

2. *Otto's philosophy of religious experience is not a theology.*

What is unforgivable in Otto's study is his use of terms whose conventional meaning he does not retain. In the Foreword to this study, he declares, "I have ventured to write of that which may be called 'non-rational' or 'supra-rational' *in the depths of the divine nature.*" (18) But this is certainly not what he has done, if "divine nature" is construed as a term to designate a reality transcendent of human experience.

Otto uses the same terms to designate experience which others use to designate a reality other than experience. Yet, he disavows any referential function of experience beyond experience itself; and he does so because he begins his analysis of experience with the dogmatic Kantian theory that the objects of warranted knowledge-claims are experiences.

His own criticism of other philosophers is instructive. He upbraids Schopenhauer and also Fichte, for using terms such as "energy" and "will" to designate "real qualifications of" a "non-rational" reality existing apart from experience. (19) But Otto is consistent with Kant's dogmatic theory of knowledge, and therefore he repudiates as unwarranted any interpretation of a reality which is transcendent of experience. Yet, this very dogmatic dualism makes Otto incapable of analyzing religious faith. Religious faith is a conviction that knowledge is possible of a reality existing transcendent of experience, and it is the confidence that human life is able to know something of a divine authority by which man ought to live.

3. *The Kantian theory of knowledge discredits religious faith.*

By means of his empirical criterion for warranted knowledge-claims, Kant proposed to set limits to the extravagances of dogmatism in philosophy, in theology, and in speculative science. This project is indeed eminently praiseworthy, for as Kant himself declared, the upshot of "wandering inadvertently beyond objects of experience" has been floundering "into the field of chimeras". (20) Yet, it is this delimitation of knowledge-claims to experience itself which discredits not only pretensions to a knowledge, which may well be considered "illusions"; it also discredits the undertaking to know something of realities which exist external to experience. And yet, it may be said that if, and when, we know something of their natures, we will have attained an informed science of the physical world; and an informed theology, as an interpretation of the nature of a reality which religious faith affirms is transcendent of the physical world.

This presupposition, however, defines for us an objective in life. It is to learn more than we already assume to know of the physical world in which we live; and to learn more of the divine reality upon which we venture to believe we are ultimately dependent for a "wisdom which needing no light, enlightens the minds that need it." (21)

5

EMPIRICAL ANALYSIS AS ANTI-THEOLOGICAL

IF THERE is one point of view which is representative of contemporary empirical philosophies of language analysis, it is Logical Positivism. According to Logical Positivism, a statement which is not verifiable is "metaphysical", and conversely, a metaphysical statement is "in principle unverifiable." (1) A statement is said to be unverifiable when "there is no cognitive criterion for deciding" whether the affirmation of a statement is warranted, or whether its negation is warranted. A statement, furthermore, whose knowledge-value cannot be ascertained is said to be "insignificant". It is insignificant whether it is affirmed, or whether it is denied: nothing more is known about a reality other than the statement in either case.

That there are many such purely verbal statements in the histories of philosophy, science, and religion cannot be denied. But, it is a matter of grave concern when an analyst of language maintains that all metaphysical statements are purely verbal.

Theology is a metaphysic, and so when *all* metaphysical statements are said to be purely verbal, it follows that all theologies are regarded as "merely word systems". (2)

But a purely verbal system, to use a description of Ogden and Richards, is "symbolically starved". (3) It is symbolically starved in the sense that its language does not refer beyond itself. When theologies, therefore, are said to be "symbolically starved", all theological statements are dismissed as words without informative function.

According to Logical Positivism, the language in theology is only expressive: it expresses how man feels, or as Hobbes declared centuries ago, when man uses the terms "most high", "most holy", he does not affirm the nature of God. He affirms "how much we admire Him". (4)

According to Positivism as an extreme form of Empiricism, nothing can be known of a reality transcendent of experience. Any statement, therefore, about the nature of a divine reality is dismissed as "cognitively" insignificant. It may express desire; or as Hobbes declared, a statement in theology may express "how ready we would be to obey Him; which is a sign of (our) humility and of (our) will to honour Him as much as we can."

But according to this psychological analysis of an extreme empirical philosophy, nothing is said in theology about a divine reality: what is said is only about our reactions. Language in theology expresses emotion, and so it is said that theological statements are purely "emotive": they are not "assertions whose truth or falsity could be rationally argued." (5)

According to this anti-metaphysical point of view, the statement, for example, "God is good", is only descriptive of our feeling. It affirms a preference: not a proposition. It expresses an evaluation: not information about a reality other than the individual's own approbation. Hence, in keeping with this point of view, Ogden and

Richards declare that "it ought to be impossible to talk about . . . religion as though (it) were capable of giving 'knowledge'!" (6) The one function of language in religious life is evocative: it evokes "attitudes, moods, desires, feelings, emotions". According to this point of view, the concern in religious life should consequently be confined to the practical effectiveness of language to bring about certain desired responses, or as they say, "in evocative speech the essential consideration is the character of the attitude aroused". (7)

That a great amount of language employed in religious institutions serves no cognitive function can hardly be denied. A common function of language in religious institutions is to express feeling, or evoke feeling. The hymn, for example, "We praise Thee, we glorify Thee, we give thanks to Thee" declares nothing about the divine reality: it rather affirms how an individual responds in the religious service. The invitation "come unto the Lord with thanksgiving", likewise, affirms nothing of the nature of God: its function is directive, or "volitional-motivational". (8)

Yet, after this function of language in religious life has been acknowledged, it is certainly dogmatic to maintain that no other function is performed in the use of language in religious life. A statement of faith, such as a creed, may well bring about certain responses, but the evoking of a response is not the only intended function of a creed. A creed is formulated by a religious individual to state his faith: it is a statement of an interpretation of the divine reality to which he believes he relates himself in his worship. The assumed function of language in a statement of faith is for a religious individual, therefore, cognitive: it is assumed that statements of faith express

57

an interpretation of the nature of divine reality. But such an assumption is that language can be used for making metaphysical statements. (9) Yet, it is this very function of language which is discredited by every consistent empiricism, and by Logical Positivism as the most dogmatic of all contemporary anti-theological philosophies.

This dogmatic repudiation of the cognitive function of language in religious life follows as a consequence of an equally dogmatic premise that nothing can be known other than experience. According to this empiricist point of view, language may be used to state an interpretation of experience, but not an interpretation of a reality transcendent of experience. The "logical" consequence of this position is that no statements in theology are informative of the nature of a divine reality; they are informative only of experience. But empiricist philosophies of language-analysis begin with the presupposition that all warranted knowledge-claims must be limited to experience, and consequently they discredit every claim to knowledge of a reality transcendent of experience. Although logically consistent, this is nevertheless dogmatic. (10) In agreement with the presuppositions of Empiricism, one is entitled to maintain that he knows experience; but he is not equally entitled to affirm that when experience is known, nothing else can be known.

According to Empiricism, one is not "aware" in his experience of a reality other than experience. Most individuals, however, believe that there is a reality "of which" they have awareness, and they assume that some of their experiences substantiate their belief that there is a reality external to experience. Statements in physical science, for example, are commonly regarded as interpretations of a reality assumed to exist external to experiences. But this is, of course, an assumption, and there is no way to "verify" it. It is a point of view with which experiences are interpreted.

Although "inductive metaphysics is risky", as all Empiricists maintain, it is no more "risky" than any generalization in science about a physical reality. Hence it is dogmatic to affirm that "inductive metaphysics is . . . the . . . disreputable extreme of science." (11) The generalizations in science about the nature of a physical reality external to experience can no more be "verified" than can metaphysical statements. Both may, however, be substantiated in one degree or another. That the generalizations of physical science may be substantiated more completely than can some of the statements in some metaphysics depends entirely upon which scientific statements one is speaking about, and also about which metaphysical statements he is speaking. The assertion, therefore, that "if the statement is experimentally verifiable, then it is by definition empirical, not metaphysical" (12) is a definition, and an indefensible one, because the term "empirical" is ambiguous.

If the empirical test of a statement means that evidence in experience can be cited to verify a statement, then there is no warrant to make a radical distinction between scientific statements and metaphysical statements. To maintain, therefore, that all metaphysical statements are non-empirical in distinction to the empirical character of all scientific statements is simply unwarranted, since there is no less of an induction from experience to the nature of a reality other than experience in physical science than there is in metaphysics. (13)

"Inductive metaphysics is . . . risky" indeed. (14) But every induction is, and the generalizations in physical science are all inductions. Every statement in physical science which affirms an interpretation of a reality external to experience is an induction. The positivistic principle therefore which warns against inductively projecting beyond experience to the nature of a divine reality external to experience must also be adhered to in evaluating generalizations in physical science. Physical science is in the same boat as is metaphysics: there is no empirical means to know that a statement in physical science is an informed interpretation of a reality external to experience, just as there is no means to know that a statement in a metaphysic is informed of a reality external to experience. But if metaphysical statements are to be discredited on the basis of a principle that from experience nothing may be inferred about the nature of a reality external to experience, then statements in physical science must be discredited on the same basis, and it is arbitrary to do otherwise.

A rejection of metaphysics is on the basis of a presupposition; just as the acceptance of statements in physical science is also on the basis of a presupposition. When it is assumed that there is a reality external to experience of whose nature one has some information in his experience, experience is cited as the evidence from which to conclude the informed character of the interpretation. But this is circular; it is first assumed that there is a reality of whose nature something is known by means of experience. From experience, one then concludes something about the nature of the reality he assumes to exist transcendent of his experience. Yet, if one didn't assume something of its nature, he would have no point of view with which to select from among his experiences those which he believes inform him of it, and those which do not.

1. *Every interpretation of experience is from the point of view of some presupposition.*

On the basis of presuppositions about the nature of realities external to experience, experiences themselves are evaluated for their informative character. Thus there is no way one can escape the function of a presupposition in interpreting experience, and this fact is well illustrated in Descartes' analysis.

In his *Meditations on the First Philosophy*, Descartes proposed "to establish a firm and abiding" "superstructure (for) the sciences" (15), and to accomplish this, he proposed an analysis "of the principles on which (his) . . . beliefs rested". (16) One belief he held in common with almost everyone else is that there is a physical reality external to experience. But, he admits that there is no evidence within experience to make it necessary to believe that there is such a reality. That there is any reality external to experience is a conjecture, or a presupposition. When it is assumed that there is a reality external to "sensory experience", some sensory experiences are interpreted as evidence for its reality, but unless its reality is first assumed, no sensory experience could possibly be appealed to as evidence that there is something external to experience itself.

The data of experience do not include the existence of a reality apart from experience. Whatever is believed about such a reality rests upon the assumption that external to experience is a reality of which something may be known from experience. This assumption, however, is a point of view with which the referential function of experience is interpreted. But the warrant for this assumption cannot be established by an appeal to experience: since the assumption is a point of view with which experiences are interpreted.

Consistent with an empiricist's point of view, Descartes declares that one imagines there is a "body" other than his experience, and he cautiously adds, "in imagining it, (the mind) turns towards the body, and contemplates in it" some property which conforms to its idea of it *"if it is true that there are bodies"*. (17) But that there are physical entities existing external to experience is, as Descartes soundly points out, a presupposition. Thus the existence of a reality external to experience is not in the same class of knowledge-claims as are statements about experience. Experiences are "first person" data: the existence of a reality external to experience is not a "first person" datum.

That there is a reality external to experience is a realistic presupposition, and it is a point of view which supplements the empiricist premise. Experience is known, as the empiricist affirms, but the realist affirms that more than experience is known by means of experience. That an individual is acquainted with his experience is the premise of every empiricism. That an individual may be acquainted with a reality external to his experience is a premise of some realistic theories of knowledge.

The existence of a reality external to experience, as is presupposed by realistic theories, is not strictly an inference from experience, since a reality external to experience is not included in experience. If, however, it is assumed that there is a reality external to experience, something of which one is acquainted in his experience, then something of its nature may be inferred from some experiences. It is inferred, however, only because it is at first assumed that some experiences are *of* a reality external to experience. But if this is not assumed, experience itself is all that may be claimed as knowledge.

Descartes, therefore, is a consistent empiricist when he declares that there is no principle whatever for escaping a thoroughgoing skepticism toward all knowledge-claims about anything other than experiences. But as soon as the presupposition is made that there is something other than experience which is known in experience, one is no longer an empiricist. Descartes, consequently, is a consistent empiricist when he cautiously declares that "I do not find that, from the idea of a physical body . . . I can necessarily infer the existence of any body." (18) According to the premise of empiricism, what is known is experience, and consistent with this point of view, Descartes declares that "there is exceedingly little which is known with certainty respecting corporeal objects." (19) This should, however, be stated even more strongly: according to a strict empiricism, nothing is known *for certain* about the nature of any reality external to experience. What is known, according to empiricism, is experience, and as a consequence of this presupposition, it follows, as Descartes points out, that "all the . . . sciences that have for their end the consideration of (physical) bodies, are indeed of a doubtful character." (20)

But after specifically proposing an empiricist point of view for his philosophical analysis, Descartes smuggled in the realistic presupposition when he said "of those objects I had no knowledge beyond what the ideas themselves gave me." (21) It is obvious that beginning with an analysis of his experience, *as his experience,* he could not even have an idea that there are objects external to his experience. The notion that there are such objects is an assumption with which experiences are interpreted, and it is this assumption which Descartes never doubted, even when he proposed to employ the method of strict empiricism.

That there may be nothing other than experience is, of course, theoretically possible. Descartes is aware of this, and admits that "perhaps there might be found in me some faculty, though hitherto unknown to me", which produces these "ideas" of a reality external to sensory experience. (22) With sound insight into the requirements of his own method, confined within the limits of strict empiricism, he asks, "What is there then that can be esteemed true?" He confesses, "perhaps this only, that there is absolutely nothing certain." (23) What he means, of course, is that beginning with the premise of strict empiricism, and interpreting experiences *as experiences,* there is no basis whatsoever to be certain that one knows anything other than experience.

2. *Descartes' belief that there is a reality external to experience is a presupposition.*

Descartes, therefore, is a consistent empiricist in so far as he maintains that the existence of "the earth, the sky, the stars" external to his "perceiving by the senses" is "doubtful". (24) But it is doubtful only when one begins an analysis of experience with the premise that *all* warranted knowledge-claims must be limited to experience. Although Descartes proposes to limit his knowledge-claims to statements of which he could be "certain", he does, however, make claims to a knowledge of realities which are external to his experience. He assumes, for

64

example, the informative function of statements about the nature of mind, and about the nature of matter. "These two ideas," he says, "seem to have this in common, that they both represent substances." (25)

But this referential function of ideas is a presupposition with which these ideas are interpreted. The idea of an extended body, and the idea of an unextended mind, must, however, be interpreted by an empiricist only as definitions. Yet, according to Descartes, they are not definitions, but propositions about realities other than experience. Descartes, therefore, is not an empiricist, and never confined his analysis of experience to the presuppositions of an empiricist. (26) He gave lip service to the empiricist point of view in his analysis of his experiences, but throughout his entire analysis he assumed the realistic point of view.

What, therefore, makes his analysis so inconsistent is the unacknowledged presuppositions with which he interpreted experience. He always assumed that his experiences informed him of something external to experiences. But this is an affirmation of faith, and it in no way follows from an analysis of experience, *as experience*. It is a point of view with which experiences are interpreted.

If, however, what Descartes affirmed about mind and body were interpreted to be only *interpretations of his idea of mind,* and *of his idea of body,* his analysis would be a consistent empiricism. But Descartes assumed that his statements about mind, and about body, affirm something of the nature of realities which are other than his experiences. (27) Thus the symbolic function of statements is a feature of language which Descartes took for granted. And yet, it is a function which may not be taken for granted. When it is assumed, the assumption must be explicitly stated as one of the presuppositions with which one begins his analysis of "first person" experience.

The belief that nothing is known in experience other than experience is one presupposition. The belief that something of a reality other than experience may be known in experience is another presupposition. The realistic presupposition, however, is defended by the individual who believes that the empiricist presupposition is not adequate to interpret experience. Yet, this preference itself expresses the conviction that there is a reality other than experience, and if it were not assumed that there is a reality other than experience, no one would defend a realistic theory of knowledge. Everyone would be a radical empiricist, for the simple reason that no one would find warrant within experience to believe that there is any reality external to experience.

Descartes assumed from the beginning of his analysis that there are realities external to his experience, and he also assumed that something of their nature can be known in his experience. (28) But he did not explicitly state either of these presuppositions. He simply took them for granted. They were, in other words, "smuggled in"; and it is for this reason that his so-called "empirical analysis" is "a begging of the question", and is not an empiricism.

3. *Descartes' belief in the reality of God is a presupposition, or faith, and it is not the result of an ontological argument.*

One of Descartes' presuppositions is that from a clear idea about a reality other than experience, one may infer that such a reality exists. He consequently infers existence from the idea of existence, because he presupposes that "objects which are clearly and distinctly conceived . . . are substances really" existent. (29)

Consistent with an empirical analysis of ideas, however, all that may be said is that when one has a clear idea, he has an idea, or, as Descartes himself soundly declares, "I can draw from my thought *the idea* of an object." (30) Yet, Descartes is not willing to limit his knowledge-claims to this cautious empiricism, and therefore he argues that "it follows that all I clearly and distinctly apprehend to pertain to this object, does in truth belong to it." (31) But, according to an empirical analysis of experience, all that may be inferred is *the idea of a reality as existing;* not the existence of a reality of which one has an idea.

Descartes began his analysis of experience with the faith that there is a reality other than experience, but he made the mistake in stipulating too restricted a basis for a defense of the knowledge-claims of this faith. From the "perfection of this idea . . . of God", for example, he argued that "God himself" is demanded as its cause. (32) This argument, however, rests upon the assumption that there is a God of which man has ideas.

Descartes further affirms that "there can be no doubt that God possesses the power of producing all the objects I am able distinctly to conceive", and although this may very well be the case, it has nothing to do with the ontological argument. This argument proposes that because "I cannot conceive God unless as existing, it follows that existence is inseparable from Him, and therefore, that He really exists." (33) These are two entirely different positions, and Descartes confused them, just as Anselm had confused them. (34) One is that God exists: the other is that there is an idea of God as existing.

It was the Renaissance confidence in the possibility of reducing all knowledge-claims to demonstrative certainty which explains the zeal with which Descartes attempted to apply the method of logic to the faith of religious life. But this attempt was made because he understood neither the nature of purely analytical statements, nor the nature of statements expressing religious faith. Had he understood either, he would never have proposed to arrive at knowledge-claims of a divine reality existing external to his ideas from an analysis of his ideas. But since he did not understand the difference of an analytic and a synthetic statement, he treated one as the other, and, therefore, argued that because he "cannot conceive God unless as existing, it follows that existence is inseparable from Him." (35)

The existence, however, of a divine reality is a religious faith: it is a belief, or presupposition, with which a religious individual interprets some of his experiences.

If, on the other hand, one begins his interpretation of experience with the presupposition that what is known is experience, he has a point of view consistent with empiricism: it is the denial of the warrant for a claim to knowledge of the nature of any reality transcendent of experience.

This skeptical discrediting of all knowledge of realities external to experience is consistent philosophizing, but it is safe to say that no person, even the most sophisticated of radical empiricists, actually believes this. Hume did not believe it. This is why he admitted that, when he left his desk on which he wrote his empiricist philosophy, his theory seemed so remote from non-theoretical experience.

No religious individual believes that his knowledge-claims are confined to his ideas. He believes that interpretations of a reality transcendent of experience may be informed of the nature of such a reality. Yet, the warrant for this faith is discredited by every empiricist theory of knowledge. Consistent with the dogmatism of an empiricist's theory of knowledge, Kant specifically declares that "we understand nothing of . . . transcendent relationships of man to the Supreme Being." (36)

4. *Schleiermacher's analysis of religious experience within the presuppositions of Kant's theory of knowledge discredits metaphysics.*

When this Kantian position is assumed as an incontestable theory of knowledge, there is no possible basis for defending religious faith as an interpretation of a divine reality. Schleiermacher, so-called "Father of Modern Protestant Theology", however, accepted Kant's theory of knowledge, and therefore interpreted religious faith as an experience: not as an experience of a reality of which there is an interpretation in experience. Yet, the object of religious faith is not experience. Religious faith is an experience, but faith is religious only when there is a trust in a reality which is believed to be completely other than experience. Schleiermacher, as an interpreter of Christian theology within the presuppositions of Kant's theory of knowledge, twists the affirmation of religious faith into a psychology of religious experience when he declares that "all the divine attributes to be dealt with in Christian Dogmatics are only meant to explain the feeling of absolute dependence". (37)

This, however, is not an analysis of religious faith: it is rather a dogmatic affirmation of what religious faith may claim to know if it is to remain consistent with an empiricist theory of knowledge. But one cannot analyze religious faith within the limits of such a theory of knowledge, since any theory of knowledge which discredits the warrant for claiming knowledge of a reality other than experience is simply incompatible with religious faith.

Religious faith is not in experience: it is in a reality believed to be transcendent of experience. It is an affirmation about a divine nature which *alone* warrants man's complete trust. But this is a metaphysical statement; and whatever is believed about this reality in religious life is a theology: it is a doctrine about the nature of the reality upon which religious life depends with an unqualified trust.

Intimidated, however, by Kant's authority in philosophy, Schleiermacher took for granted that it is philosophically unwarranted to claim knowledge of a reality transcendent of experience. Hence he maintained that a religious experience is "the consciousness of being absolutely dependent"; and in an attempt to interpret religious faith in a manner compatible with the Kantian theory of knowledge, he declared that "the consciousness of being absolutely dependent is precisely the same thing as the consciousness of being in relation to God." (38) But this is to affirm that a religious individual is aware of his experience, and not of the nature of God in his religious experience. (39)

Schleiermacher was preoccupied with experience, as if this were the only reality of which anything could be known, or of which any knowledge-claim may justifiably be made. Yet, in spite of this, he has enjoyed a wide influence in Protestant Theology for more than a century. This may in part be accounted for by the ambiguity in

his analysis, and Professor H. R. Mackintosh has soundly pointed out that "it is impossible not to feel that the
ambiguity served him well, and that at various points his
argument would have broken down irretrievably had
the ambiguity been cleared up." (40) It may, therefore,
be safe to say, if Schleiermacher's analysis of religious
faith had been subjected to a sound scrutiny many years
ago, the tradition of Protestant Theology in the western
world might have been saved a detour into one of the
most arid deserts in which one could lose his way.

Religious experience is a faith in a reality which is
believed to be completely worthy of man's trust, and because it is believed to be worthy of trust, man turns to it
for a help which he does not believe can be found within
the resources of his life, or within the physical world. But
Schleiermacher could not speak about a completely dependable reality in which religious faith trusts, for this
would be a metaphysic. He therefore speaks of the experience of "complete dependence". Yet, the feeling of complete dependence is not necessarily a religious experience:
what alone makes it a religious experience is the faith
that there is a completely dependable reality upon which
one may with warrant completely depend.

Thus there is no religious faith without a theology.
A theology is simply an interpretation of the completely
dependable reality in which one has faith; and to speak
about religious faith without a theology is a contradiction. Whereas "a sense of absolute dependence" is a psychological description of experience, a faith that there is
a reality upon which one may completely depend, because it is completely dependable, is a theological statement. It is an interpretation of a reality transcendent of

life; and without such a metaphysic, there is no religious faith.

No religious individual believes that his experience constitutes the source of his security. The source of his security is the reality in which he believes, and to which he orients his life in complete trust. Hence he wants to know the nature of this reality. But this imposes upon him the necessity to discriminate between many diverse statements of faith; and religious faith itself is the conviction that there are criteria by which such a discrimination can be made, provided men were to have an informed interpretation of the divine reality.

A belief about the nature of a divine reality is, therefore, not the criterion by which a religious individual proposes to select from among competing claims to knowledge those beliefs which are true. An earnest religious individual wants to know the divine reality, and yet, his earnestness is not a sufficient condition for selecting true beliefs from among other beliefs which may be held with equal earnestness. Earnestness is a condition for learning, but it is not a criterion by which the truth-character of beliefs can be ascertained.

According to religious faith, the criterion for the truth-character of interpretations of the divine reality is a knowledge of the divine reality. But this criterion of religious faith imposes a task upon a religious individual. It confronts him with a life-long quest: it is to know of the divine reality "as much as he can receive, wisdom in proportion to his thirst." (41)

6

THE PROJECTION BEYOND EXPERIENCE

IN HIS attempt to be an empiricist, Kant maintains that we know the features of our experience. But he maintains, as no empiricist consistently can, that there is a reality other than experience.

As an empiricist, Kant may maintain that what is known are experiences, but he may not say that there are "things as objects of our senses existing outside us (as) given". (1) This is not a statement about the features of experience: it is rather an interpretation of their causation by a reality external to experience. Such an interpretation obviously presupposes a metaphysic as much as any other theory of knowledge which makes no pretense to being empirical.

Kant, however, attempted to limit knowledge-claims to an empiricist's point of view even though he did not begin his analysis of experience with an empiricist's point of view. And it is this inconsistency which accounts for the ambiguity in his terminology. He speaks, for example, of organized experiences as "appearances" of "things", and yet, he maintains that no reality apart from experiences "appears" *in* experience. It is therefore inconsistent to claim that there is a causal factor external to sen-

73

sation in order to account for sensations, and then to claim that no features of experience *in any way* inform one of this reality. It is enough to maintain, as an empiricist does, that knowledge must be confined to experience, without presuming to say, as Kant does, that we can know that no properties of a reality existing external to experience are as they "appear" to us to be. The statement, therefore, that "they represent in no respect . . . anything more than mere appearance of those things, but never their constitution", (2) reveals the dogmatism with which Kant interpreted experience.

In interpreting experience, Kant wants to follow the point of view of an empiricist, yet he argues that since all experiences are organized, there must be organizing forms which are other than organized experiences. In making this distinction, however, he introduces a dualism between experiences and what is other than experiences, and consequently, after importing this dualism of organized experiences and organizing forms, he has two very different realities for which to account.

Kant did not merely give an empirical description of the features of experience; he also sought to account for these features; and in doing this, he began with the presuppositions of a dogmatic realist, and a dogmatic rationalist. He assumes that there is a reality other than experience, and so presumed that there is a causation for some experiences which is external to experience. He likewise assumed that the organization of experiences is a contribution exclusively of the individual, and so discloses no property of a reality external to experience.

If, however, Kant had begun his analysis of experience as an empiricist, he would never have imported these concepts of traditional metaphysics into his analysis. But the more vigorously he disavows metaphysics, the more obvious it is that there are metaphysical presuppositions at the basis of his analysis. What, therefore, makes his theory of knowledge philosophically weak is his denunciation of metaphysics when the basis of his theory of knowledge is a metaphysic.

To explain why there is organized experience is not an empiricist's project; it is rather the proposal of one who assumes that in experience, more than experience itself is known. The explanatory factor for organizing experience is not itself any organized experience. If one were to describe experiences, as a consistent empiricist proposes to do, nothing could be claimed as knowledge about a pure form, and a formless content. These abstractions are not features of any analyzed experiences. They are rather assumptions with which Kant analyzes experiences, and then justifies these assumptions on the ground that they enable him to understand the nature of experience. But what Kant claims to know in his analysis is not only experience: it is also an explanation of why there are experiences which are organized as they are found to be organized.

1. *Inferences are made from experience to the properties of a reality other than experience.*

No belief about the existence of a reality external to experience, however, would ever be ventured if it were not first assumed that there is something other than experience. The existence of such a reality is not inferred from experience: it is assumed, and the assumption that there is such a reality is the point of view with which some experiences are interpreted.

A claim to know that there is any correlation between

features of experiences, and the properties of a reality other than experience, is a faith. It is a faith that there is a reality other than experience, and it is also a faith that some experiences are informative of its nature. Without this faith, experiences would have to be construed as an empiricist proposes they should be: they alone would be regarded as the given which is known.

If sensory experiences, for example, were accepted as the given, and no claim were made to knowledge of sensible properties of a physical reality, then, and only then, would sensory experiences be analyzed consistently with an empiricist's premise. They woud be regarded as events, and not as events referring beyond themselves. But the fact that some experiences are regarded as referring to something beyond themselves is the "realistic" assumption.

An empiricist, however, would acknowledge that there is such an assumption, but he would not presume to pass judgment on its warrant unless he were to become inconsistent with his premise. He could not pass judgment upon the warrant for any inference from experience to a reality other than experience, because he cannot pass judgment upon the warrant for assuming that there is a reality other than experience whose properties are in some way correlated with experiences.

No one, therefore, may claim to be an empiricist when he presumes to say that knowledge-claims about the sensible properties of a physical world are warranted, whereas claims to a knowledge of a divine reality other than the physical world are not warranted. In so far as both the physical world, and the divine reality are transcendent of experience, both of these realities are in the same category in so far as knowledge-claims are concerned. To assume that properties of a physical world can be known in experience is no less of an assumption, or faith, than is the belief that something of the nature of a divine reality transcendent of the physical world can be known.

The warrant, however, for the faith that there is a physical world, as well as the warrant for the faith that there is a divine reality transcendent of the physical world, does not depend upon any experiences from which their reality may be inferred. It depends rather upon the truth of the belief that there is a physical world, and a divine reality.

If there is a reality to which some experiences refer, the interpretation of some experiences as referring to such a reality is a true interpretation; and if there is no such reality, the interpretation is false. (3) In neither case, however, could an empiricist, if he is consistent, venture any comment, since he presumes to know experience, and nothing of a reality other than experience.

Philosophical empiricism may be said to be a point of view with which experiences are interpreted when a minimum of faith is involved. The only venture of faith which a strict empiricist in scientific procedure requires is the assumption that there will be other experiences to which present experiences may be correlated; and the assumption that what is known about present experiences is on the basis of what has been learned from past experiences. But if these beliefs about past and future experiences are not granted as warranted presuppositions, an empiricist can consistently claim to know nothing: he can only aesthetically enjoy a present experience.

If, however, it is assumed that there have been past

experiences of which something is known in the present: and if it is also assumed that there may be future experiences, then even an empiricist is not without faith. But, if one must admit the element of faith even in claiming to know something of past experience, it ought not be too excessive a strain to admit that a faith in a physical reality other than experience might be ventured as warranted. Just where the warrant for faith must end is, of course, a problem. In fact, it is the whole problem in a theory of knowledge.

2. *A belief in the existence of a reality other than experience is not an inference.*

Few individuals with a knowledge of scientific studies would today hesitate to assume an atomic structure of the physical world. And yet, the existence of such an atomic structure is not inferred from any sensory experiences. When, however, it is assumed that there are structures which emit energy, and when it is further assumed that such radiations of energy can be detected, then it is assumed that something is known of an atomic structure. But this is very indirect reasoning; and yet, it is the same indirect reasoning which is involved in all knowledge-claims of any reality other than the data of experience.

An analysis of physical bodies in terms of atoms cannot appeal to sensory experience for its warrant, since the very interpretation of marks on a photographic plate as evidence for an atom is an interpretation of sensory data from the point of view that there is an atomic structure. Atoms are assumed to exist, and certain visual data are interpreted as manifestations of energy radiations from atoms. (4) Yet, the very claim to know something about atomic structure rests upon the elementary assumption that what cannot be directly perceived, nevertheless, may exist.

Interpretations of the properties of an atom are assumptions with which certain sensory data are interpreted. From the observed features of oil-droplets between charged plates, something is assumed as knowledge about the properties of electrons. But this claim to knowledge of the properties of electrons is not an inference from visual data. Rather, some visual data are interpreted as informative of an electron's properties in a certain context, when the nature of an electron is first assumed. With this assumption, or point of view, some visual data are interpreted as referring to events which are accounted for as effects of an electron. But the evidence of visual data for an electron is an interpretation of visual experience from the point of view of an hypothesis about atomic structure.

Assumptions such as this would never become problems in philosophical analysis if the warrant for inference did not itself constitute one of the problems of reflective life. When, however, inference becomes a problem in a philosophical analysis of experience, one becomes aware that much which passes for "experience" is simply assumptions taken for granted as the very conditions for interpreting experience. When, therefore, these assumptions are clarified, one becomes aware that very little is "empirically given".

When, for example, one concludes from experiences that there are realities other than experience, he takes more for granted than experience: he also takes for granted the point of view with which he interprets experiences. Such a point of view is specifically taken for granted when, from relations within experience, something is assumed as knowledge of correlated relations in a physical world. From an awareness only of relations in experience, nothing would be inferred about relations between objects external to experience, unless the existence of such objects were first assumed. This assumption, however, is taken for granted in the inference of "physical space" from "perceptual space"; and unless the assumption were made that there is a correlation between relations in percepts and relations in a physical reality, nothing would be claimed as knowledge of relations in a physical reality.

When from experiences, something is assumed to be known about a reality external to experience, an assumption is made about the correlation of features of experiences, and properties of realities which are other than experiences. When such a correlation is assumed, it is then also assumed that there is a causal connection between experiences and a reality other than experiences. But it is only when one assumes that there is a causal connection that one infers something of the properties of a reality other than his experiences from the features of his experiences. This inference, therefore, is not simply a deduction from experience: it is rather a deduction from the assumption that there is a reality other than experience of which something is known by means of experience.

The fact that this is taken for granted by nearly everyone does not in the least lessen the fact that it is an assumption with which experiences are interpreted; and that by no stretch of careless language can it be said that the existence of a physical reality is "empirically given" in sensory experience. Sensory experiences to which attention is given are, however, so constantly construed to be informative of a reality other than experience, that the assumptions involved in this interpretation are not even taken into account.

Such a claim to a knowledge of a reality other than experience, on the basis of what is known in experience, is an instance of habitual induction, and the warrant for induction as a procedure is habitually taken for granted. If induction, however, were merely described as a procedure in interpreting experiences, there would be no philosophical problem. It is only when an induction is made from experience, which an empiricist describes, to a reality other than experience, that the warrant for induction arises as a philosophical problem.

Experiences may be described in an empirical analysis, but realities which are assumed to be other than experiences cannot be described without first making the assumptions about the informative character of experience. When such description is attempted, however, features of experiences are assumed to be correlated with properties other than experience, and it is this assumption which constitutes a theoretical problem. Yet, this problem arises only when experience is analyzed from the point of view that there is something other than experience. If experience itself were assumed to be the object of knowledge, this problem of induction would not arise.

From an awareness of the features of one experience, an empiricist predicts the occurrence of subsequent experiences with comparable features. Yet, when such recurrence of features in experience is predicted, the warrant for prediction likewise becomes a problem even for an empiricist.

Induction is not simply an assumption: it is a procedure based upon assumptions. Hence, the inductive procedure cannot be justified by an appeal to experiences, since experiences which are cited to justify the procedure have already been interpreted from the point of view that the procedure is justified.

When confronted by this procedure, one must admit that it cannot be justified, since it is the very procedure used in arguing a justification. If there is one principle, therefore, which must be taken for granted, it is the principle of induction: it is the procedure of passing beyond the data of a present attention either in predicting comparable experiences, or in claiming to know something of a reality external to experience. If, however, the claim to a knowledge of the properties of a reality external to experience is not warranted from the data of experience, then the prediction of the occurrence of another experience comparable to a present experience is likewise not justified. In either case, there is a "leap" from one thing to something else, and without this procedure, nothing could be claimed as knowledge. All attention would be confined to the features of a present experience.

But even the empiricists are not satisfied to settle for this little. To do so would reduce empiricism to a solipsism, and thus a skepticism toward every knowledge-claim beyond the moment. This would not only be a repudiation of science: it would also be a repudiation of the possibility for articulating such a philosophy. Unless, therefore, induction is accepted as a procedure—even though it cannot be justified by an appeal to experience—no interpretation of experience is possible. An interpretation of experience, even as experience, is the correlation of one experience with another, and such correlation is a classification. One experience, however, cannot be classified with another unless both are regarded as instances of a type, and this very classification is an inductive procedure.

3. *The belief that there is a reality other than experience is an assumption.*

Every interpretation of experience is from some point of view, and an empiricist regards the reference beyond experience itself simply as a point of view. Although it is a point of view, to be sure, no empiricist may, however, without dogmatism maintain that there is nothing to this point of view other than a peculiarity of experience.

According to an empiricist, the belief that there is a reality is an experience, and it is not a point of view for interpreting the nature of something other than experience. The empiricist's point of view cannot indeed be discredited by a non-empiricist's point of view any more than a non-empiricist's point of view can be discredited by the empiricist's point of view. These are two points of view with which experiences may be interpreted, and the difference of an empiricist's point of view, and a non-empiricist's point of view, constitutes a fundamental difference in a theory about experience. When an empiricist analyzes experiences, he believes that experiences are known. When a non-empiricist analyzes experiences, he assumes that a reality other than experiences may be known by means of experience.

It is obvious that "experience" does not mean the same in both theories of knowledge. For the empiricist, an analysis of experience discloses peculiarities of experience: for a non-empiricist, an analysis of experience may be an interpretation of the nature of something other than experience. These two theories of knowledge are not confused about the term "experience". Each is clear about the term, but each uses the term to designate a different object of knowledge, and each uses "object of knowledge" in different ways.

That the term "perception" designates an experience is indeed a matter merely of terminology, but it is not just a matter of terminology to distinguish "perception of experience", and "perception of something other than experience". This distinction is a matter of propositions about the knowledge significance of experience, and it is not merely a matter of defining the term "experience".

As a matter of fact, a definition of this term can be stated only after a theory of knowledge has first been presupposed. When one assumes that the object of knowledge is itself experience, he defines experience as an event informative of experience. When, however, one assumes that the object which is known in experience may be something other than experience, he speaks of some experiences as possibly informative of a reality other than experience.

A strict empiricist does not, of course, attempt to analyze the warrant for assuming that there is information of a reality other than experiences. He takes it for granted that there is no warrant for this assumption. A non-empiricist, on the other hand, sees no warrant to discredit the belief that there is something other than experience, and he looks upon the empiricist as pre-judging experience by his premise that what is known is experience, and nothing other than experience. This is the deadlock in philosophical analysis, and it cannot be resolved in the contest of the empiricist and the non-empiricist theories of knowledge.

The basis for the difference of empiricist and non-empiricist theories of knowledge is with the interpretation of what may be claimed as knowledge in experience. According to the empiricist, experience is known: not something other than it. According to the non-empiricist, some experiences may refer to a reality which is other than experience, and so something of its nature may be known in experience.

4. *The claim to a knowledge of a reality external to experience is a projection beyond experience.*

Relations in experience may be described as experiences, even when no claim to a knowledge of any reality other than experience is made. When, however, relations within experience are taken to be informative of relations between objects other than experience, more than experience is appealed to in making this claim. Visual experiences, for example, may be interpreted as pointing to physical stars. But a belief in the existence of stars as sources from which energy radiates to the human eye is as much a projection beyond experience, as is the belief that each star is a gravitational center. The interpretation of a physical star in terms of a gravitational center is, however, not an interpretation of sensory experiences. It is rather an interpretation of the nature of a reality of which it is assumed one has awareness in some sensory experiences.

This interpretation cannot be explained in terms of sensory experiences, since what the properties of a star are believed to be are projections beyond sensory experience. They are interpretations not of experiences: but of realities of whose properties something is assumed to be known in some experiences, and if it were not for the interpretation of the nature of realities external to experience, nothing would be claimed as knowledge except the features of experience.

When, however, it is assumed that there are bodies external to experiences, experiences are interpreted in a way that they would not be interpreted if this assumption were not made. And this assumption itself accounts for the difference between speaking of "perceptions as experiences" and "perceptions as experiences of a reality other than experience".

From what is assumed to be the properties of a reality other than experience, inferences are made about the knowledge-value of experience. It is inferred that since there are realities with certain properties, these properties are experienced when there are experiences with certain features. Yet, the correlation of features in experience with properties of a reality other than experience is an inference secondary to a projection. It is only when a reality beyond experience is assumed, and experiences are interpreted from the point of view of this assumption, that features of experience are construed to be correlated with properties of a reality other than experience.

Without this assumption, experiences might be analyzed as experiences, but they could not be analyzed as informative of something other than experience. What is claimed of such realities from the data of experience is determined by what is thought about the nature of such realities. When, for example, one speaks of his "perception of a star", or his "perception of a planet", the properties he claims to know of either star or planet on the evidence of his sensory experiences, are consistent with what he assumes about their nature. What is perceived in both cases, however, are only luminous dots in relation to other luminous dots, but some of these dots are interpreted from the point of view that there are planets which move in elliptical orbits about the sun. Other data are interpreted as perceptions of stars which exist outside the solar system. Nothing, however, of the nature either of planets or stars is disclosed in sensory data. It is rather that one fits his visual experiences into an interpretation of the world, and the ones he fits into his interpretation are interpreted from the point of view of the hypothesis of the nature of the world.

The claim to knowledge that our galaxy consists of three hundred thousand millions of stars is, for example, not based on perceptions. It is an hypothesis about the cosmic context of our earth with which some perceptions are interpreted. No one, even with the help of the Hale telescope, would speak of perceiving this vast universe. What is perceived on photographs with the two hundred inch telescope are luminous pin points, and these pin points are interpreted as vast bodies at incredible distances from the earth. A reading of a photograph of the heavens is an interpretation of luminous points in a visual field as correlations with bodies in a physical field, whose vast totality constitutes the physical world.

What is claimed as knowledge of the physical world from the reading of photographs is, therefore, not an inference from the photographs. The photographs, rather, are interpreted from the point of view of the hypothesis of the vast world with its millions of stars, and its countless galaxies. Thus the visual data acquired in reading photographs do not constitute a knowledge comprising astronomy: knowledge in astronomy consists of propositions about the nature of physical bodies—planets, stars, and galaxies—and these are not inferences from sensory data, but are hypotheses with which sensory data are interpreted.

The difference, therefore, in modern and ancient astronomies is not primarily the advance of the modern photographic telescope. It is rather the point of view of the modern astronomer who interprets photographs; since even modern photographs in the hands of the ancients would have been interpreted just as the ancients interpreted the visual data of the unaided eye.

What may be said about the projective character beyond experience in the interpretations of astronomy may also be said about religious faith. A religious faith that "the heavens declare the glory of God" is an interpretation of the source of the physical world. It is not an interpretation of visual data: it is an interpretation of the significance of the physical world in a divine purpose. But even the belief in a physical world is an interpretation; not of experience, but of a reality other than experience; and with this interpretation, certain experiences are in turn interpreted as informative of some of its properties. The belief in a physical world, as well as the belief in a divine creator of the physical world, are projections beyond experiences; and both beliefs are expressions of the faith with which some experiences are interpreted.

7

INTERPRETATIONS AS CONSTRUCTS

THE assumptions with which experiences are interpreted are "constructs"; and there is no interpretation of any experience without such constructs.

When this function of constructs, or complex assumptions, is acknowledged in the interpretation of sensory experiences, one cannot help but be impressed with the naive analysis proposed by the empiricist Locke: "he that would not deceive himself ought to build his hypothesis on matter of fact, and make it out by sensible experience." (1)

One need only examine a few of the hypotheses, or complex assumptions, in empirical science to become aware of the non-sensory source for the concepts with which the physical world is interpreted.

1. *Constructs are interpretations.*

Galileo's law, for example, that in a medium of zero density, physical bodies fall with equal acceleration, is not a statement about sensory experiences, and it is not even a generalization based on the evidence of actual observations. It is, rather, an interpretation of an ideal situation, which it was not even experimentally possible for Galileo to create.

Yet, without a vacuum, Galileo formulated this principle, and with this principle as an hypothesis, he made corrections in the data he observed. But, such corrections would never have been ventured were it not for the principle itself he proposed. This is, of course, circular. The hypothesis stipulates which corrections in observed data must be taken into account in order to substantiate the principle.

This circular procedure, however, seems to run counter to what popular opinion construes as "empirical verification". Yet, notwithstanding popular opinion, such is the procedure in an empirical verification of this hypothesis, as well as in the empirical verification of other hypotheses in science.

Galileo, it must be pointed out, did not observe the constant rate of acceleration of bodies. The constant rate of such acceleration of bodies, irrespective of their weight, is a property of bodies only in an ideal context. But Galileo did not observe bodies in an ideal context. He did however, have the intelligence to interpret falling bodies from the point of view of the hypothesis he proposed, and with this hypothesis he then made the corrections which alone could make observations compatible with his hypothesis.

Individuals who regard this circular procedure in physical science as "empirical," nevertheless, object to the same procedure in religious life. A religious individual may, for example, interpret the physical world as a manifestation of a creator's activity; and in some of the features of the world, he may find evidence for a divine purpose expressed in the world. The procedure obviously is circular. Yet, it has the same circular character as the procedure in the verification of Galileo's hypothesis. Galileo's hypothesis stipulates the conditions which must be fulfilled for its verification, and when conditions are so controlled, evidence then is found to confirm the hypothesis.

As another instance of this circular procedure in the empirical method of physical science, one may consider the Law of Boyle. The Law of Boyle has been regarded as a generalization applicable to *all ideal* gases, even though now it has been found to be applicable only to a few actual gases. This reduction, however, in the range of the applicability of this generalization has not persuaded scientists to withdraw the classification of "law" from this particular correlation of volume, pressure, and temperature. But to preserve the category of "law" for this correlation, the scope of its application had to be reduced.

Thus one procedure in empirical science is to select conditions to substantiate hypotheses: and when some conditions are found to be unsuited for substantiating an hypothesis, they are regarded as outside the range of the hypothesis.

This procedure is all a part of sober science in interpreting physical reality. Yet, it is a procedure which is frowned upon by some when it is employed in religious life. A religious individual, to be sure, does not cite every incident in his experience to substantiate his belief that there is a divine purpose. He rather selects from among the events in his life, those which he regards as evidence for substantiating his belief that there is a divine purpose. If some such selection were not made, faith in a divine purpose would be discredited even for a religious

91

individual. But when events are selected from the point of view that there is a divine purpose working itself out in human life, and in the physical world, the faith itself gains credibility.

The credibility of a religious interpretation, therefore, rests upon the wisdom of an individual to select events in life to be interpreted by a religious faith. If this is an arbitrary procedure, it must be acknowledged that it is the very same procedure which is regarded as warranted in physical science, since hypotheses in science retain their credibility only when their applicability is delimited.

What saves hypotheses in science from being discredited is the reduction in the scope of their application. This same principle might well be applied in human life to preserve the interpretative significance of some religious beliefs.

The belief that there is a divine purpose, and that certain events in human life are instances of its manifestation, is a faith with which events in life are interpreted. This interpretative procedure is circular, but it is no more so than the procedure in formulating and testing scientific hypotheses. The scientific hypothesis, for example, of the gravitational constant is equally circular. This hypothesis is the belief that "the acceleration of gravity (is) a constant near the surface of the earth". (2) With this belief, observable events are interpreted, and only because it is assumed that there is a constant pattern in the occurrence of events in the physical world, is the principle formulated. Yet, this is as circular as is the argument that events in human life which are instances of a divine purpose are evidences of a divine purpose. In both cases, the point of view with which an interpretation is made is itself an interpretation. If one did not have the faith that there is a divine purpose, no events in human life would be interpreted as instances of it. If, however, there is such a purpose, and if the events which are interpreted as instances of it are actually instances of it, then the individual who ventures this interpretation has a knowledge which others do not have who do not interpret such events from such a point of view. And the same may be said of the individual claiming knowledge of the physical world from certain points of view of scientific hypotheses. If one did not interpret occurrences in the physical world with the hypothesis of a gravitational constant, for example, he would never find empirical evidence for the justification of the notion of such a constant.

The individual, therefore, who like the eighteenth century astronomer, Laplace, should turn his telescope toward the heavens and declare there is no God, or divine purpose, because neither can be observed, is as profound as the person who should look into a telescope and disbelieve in the reality of a universal gravitational attraction in the physical world. Such gravitational attraction cannot be observed through a telescope, even though evidence of it might be detected by the use of a telescope. A divine purpose is likewise not the type of reality which can be focused upon by a telescope. A telescope may direct attention upon a segment of the physical world, but the significance of the segment as a fragment in a divine purpose cannot be observed in the telescope.

2. *Constructs are experiences.*

Some beliefs in the history of physical science are now recognized to be unsatisfactory interpretations of physical reality. They have, therefore, been eliminated from the knowledge-claims of present science. The history of science consists in such a revision of ideas by the introduction of other ideas which are regarded as more informed of the nature of the reality which scientists seek to know. For a time, for example, the model of the solar system was regarded as a helpful device in interpreting the properties of an atomic structure. (3) But, as more and more interpretations of wave phenomena were proposed, interpretations of the atom after an analogy to the solar system was found to be unsatisfactory. Bohr's model, however, still retains the advantage of all pictorial representations of interpretations: it makes vivid certain relationships. Yet, such relationships might, nevertheless, be characterized without the use of a model which spatializes interpretations.

There is always some difference in a model and in an interpretation of a reality which is graphically portrayed by means of the model. But when the differences in the model and in the interpretation of a reality are recognized, one is already aware of the informative inadequacy of the model. Although inadequate for "representing" a reality, a model may, nevertheless, designate a reality; an interpretation of which cannot be graphically represented in a spatial model. Under such circumstances, a model would then serve a symbolic function, just as language serves. It would designate a reality: not "copy" the reality to which it refers.

The distinction, however, between a model and a reality designated by means of a model can be made only by the individual who assumes to know something of the properties of a reality designated by the model. Only one who assumes to know a reality other than a model can be even aware that a model has symbolic functions. An individual, therefore, who confuses a model and the reality designated by it, is in the same category as the primitive who confuses signs with realities other than signs, and consequently identifies a symbol with a non-symbolic reality. This confusion is indeed an index of mentality; but the type of mentality of which this confusion is an index is not by any means confined to primitive communities.

Just as the individual who finds no deficiency in the Bohr model for symbolizing the properties of atomic structure knows little of wave phenomena, so likewise, the individual who sees no deficiency in anthropomorphic symbols for portraying the divine reality knows little of properties which would be compatible with a cosmic purpose, or a cosmic creator. But to appreciate what a reality would be in order to fulfill cosmic functions, is to have a criterion by which to realize the deficiency of all pictorial representations of the divine reality. The disparity of pictorial representations, and the divine reality in which a religious individual believes, is so vast that one readily realizes the limitations of pictorial symbols in religious life—even though he need not necessarily be convinced of equal limitations in the symbolic process, since even a reference beyond the stars to their Creator is a symbolic reference.

In any symbolic reference, one must always make a distinction between what is assumed to be known of a reality, and the reality itself of which something is assumed as knowledge. A failure to make this distinction is, indeed, a failure to understand what constitutes knowledge. An ability, however, to make this distinction is the type of intelligence which constitutes the minimum condition for science; and it is the same type of intelligence which constitutes the minimum condition for a religious individual's reverence of a divine reality in distinction to an awesome regard for the symbols by which it is designated.

The more that knowledge is claimed of a reality other than experience, the more effective must symbols be to direct attention to such a reality. Symbolizing is just the process of using symbols to draw attention to what is referred to. Symbols, therefore, not only may designate a reality to which one refers, but they may also record an interpretation of such a reality. Yet, when symbols record interpretations of a reality they direct attention not only to interpretations, but also to the reality which is interpreted. If an interpretation designated by a symbol is informed of the nature of a reality which is interpreted, then the symbol also designates such properties of the reality which is interpreted.

Symbols in science designate interpretations of the physical world; but a scientific knowledge of a physical reality does not consist of symbols. It consists rather of interpretations which are symbolically stated.

The failure, however, to realize that an interpreted reality, as well as an interpretation of a reality, may be designated by a symbol accounts for philosophical positions which maintain that what is known is only the symbol, or the symbolic construct. (4) *If,* however, a reality other than experience may be interpreted, and *if* the interpretation may be designated by a symbol, then the interpretation of such a reality is also known when the meaning of the symbol is known. If, consequently, an interpretation is informed of the nature of a non-symbolic reality, the symbols which designate the interpretation are then a shorthand designation of a knowledge of the non-symbolic reality.

Knowledge, neither in science, nor in religious life, consists of symbols. And neither scientific nor religious knowledge is even dependent upon symbols. What is dependent upon symbols is simply a statement of an interpretation of a reality.

Knowledge does not consist of symbols, but of interpretations informed of the nature of realities which one proposes to interpret. One type of such reality may be symbols; but if the nature of reality is not exhausted by symbols, then possible knowledge is likewise not necessarily confined to symbols.

Statements of interpretations in scientific and religious literature are symbolic expressions. These symbolic expressions are constructs in the sense that man constructs symbolic systems to state his interpretations. But both in physical science and in religious life, the realities whose natures are interpreted are not symbolic statements, and so are not merely constructs. (5)

Constructs are man's creations. The physical world and the divine reality are not. They are possible objects of man's knowledge, and when their nature is discovered, man will have an informed science, and an informed religious life.

8

INTERPRETATIONS STATED IN SYMBOLS

A SYMBOL may designate an experience; but it may also be used to designate an interpretation of what is believed to be other than experience. One experience, for example, may be designated "first", and another experience may be designated "second". "First" and "second" are language terms. But their significance as language terms is their designation of a certain serial order. A serial order in experience, however, is a non-symbolic condition for the very meaning of the symbols "first" and "second."

A designation of one experience by the symbol "first", and a designation of another experience by a symbol "second", are experiences, but the order of experiences is not an experience. Yet, a strict empiricist believes that ordered experiences can be satisfactorily analyzed without referring to anything other than particular experiences. This belief, of course, is not an empirical analysis of experiences, either of designation, or of naming. It is rather a presupposition about the nature of what can be known in experiences.

When an empiricist assumes that nothing other than experience can be known, it is obviously consistent for him to maintain that the range of knowledge-claims is confined to experiences. This conclusion simply follows from his premise, and so there can be no criticism of his logic. The ground for a criticism of an empiricist, however, is with his premise about the nature of what is known, and what can be known.

The premise of an empiricist is one point of view with which experiences are interpreted. But there is another point of view other than the empiricist's with which experiences may also be interpreted. This is the point of view that some experiences are responses to realities other than experience. The empiricist's position that all knowledge is confined to experience, however, is not an analysis of experience. It is rather a dogmatic presupposition about the knowledge-value of experience, and from this point of view, the empiricist argues about what cannot be known other than experience.

Consistency of argument is indeed a possibility for anyone who can think clearly within the confines of his own premise. A premise from which one argues is one possible point of view, but the possibility of a point of view is no evidence for the warrant of the point of view. Yet, it is the warrant for the empiricist's point of view which constitutes the whole problem in evaluating empiricism as a theory of knowledge, and not merely as a logically consistent analysis of a premise. If internal consistency were the only criterion for the soundness of an argument, no criticism could be directed against an empiricist's philosophy provided, of course, it were internally consistent. The evaluation of an empiricist's theory of knowledge, however, is not a problem of logic: it is rather a problem of the adequacy of an empiricist's premise to state what is known in experience.

Even in describing experiences, an empiricist must

distinguish between experiences which are regarded as referring to other experiences, and experiences which are regarded as referring to a reality assumed to be other than experience. In making this distinction, however, one becomes aware of the fact that it is dogmatic to maintain that all that is known is just experiences. If some experiences are "of something", the preposition "of" is then very significant in designating a possible object of awareness. An empiricist, however, would maintain that *an awareness* of the object to which attention is directed is itself experience. Although the argument is, indeed, consistent, it raises a metalogical problem. The problem is with the adequacy of the description of experience.

If experience may be actually described as simply an attending to experience itself, then no criticism whatsoever could be directed against an empiricist. But the adequacy of an empiricist's description of experience is just what may be contested. What is contested, therefore, in evaluating empiricism as a theory of knowledge is simply the empiricist's characterization of "the object" of claims to knowledge.

Claims to knowledge are experiences, but the object of such knowledge-claims need not necessarily be experiences. Hence, in describing experiences, one must distinguish between an interest in experience, and an interest in a reality which is assumed to be other than experience. That there is no such reality, is something an empiricist cannot claim to know—if he is to confine his claims of knowledge to experience. But what an empiricist can acknowledge is that some experiences refer beyond themselves to something which is believed to be other than experience.

Locke, for example, was aware of this reference. In

describing experiences, therefore, he distinguished experiences which are not assumed to refer beyond themselves from those which *are* assumed to refer beyond themselves. But he made an inference which is incompatible with an empirical description of experience when he declared that there *are* realities other than experience to which experiences refer. This, of course, is going beyond an empirical description of experiences. It is rather a claim to know a reality other than experience.

Locke, however, made this claim because he assumed that there is such a reality. Yet, the warrant for this assumption is not a matter of accuracy in describing experiences. The reference in experience to what is assumed to be other than experience may well be described by an empiricist as an experience. But to assume that the reference is warranted is no more within the province of an empiricist than it is within his province to assume that it is not warranted.

This reference is assumed to be warranted only when it is assumed that there is a reality, something of whose nature can be known in experience. But when this is assumed, more than experience is regarded as the object of knowledge: the object of knowledge is assumed to be that reality other-than-experience to which some experiences refer.

A language term has "a sense", or a meaning, only when it refers to what is other than itself. (1) This reference beyond itself is its symbolic significance. The basic problem of knowledge in an analysis of language is what a symbol with sense actually designates. The sense of a symbol is a language distinction, and therefore an empiricist argues that all that is known in the use of language is experience. But that to which a symbol with sense refers may also be regarded as a reality other than experience. These are entirely different theories of knowledge. According to the one, the object of knowledge is the symbol. According to the other, a symbol with a meaning refers to a reality other than language, and often to a reality other than experience.

According to the second theory, an interpretation of a reality other than experience is the sense of some symbols. The sense of a symbol is the reality it designates, and if the reality designated is an experience, then the features of an experience constitute the sense of the symbol. If, however, the reality designated by a symbol is other than experience, then such a reality is the sense of the symbol. But to maintain that there is no informed interpretation whatsoever of such a reality is a dogmatism with which language symbolism is interpreted.

Such a dogmatic theory of knowledge does not, of course, arise from an analysis of language, but from an assumption about what can be known. When it is assumed that nothing can be known of a reality other than experience, language as experience is claimed as the object of knowledge. Yet, an emphasis upon language as the object of all knowledge-claims does not follow from an analysis of experience: it is rather an expression of a dogmatic theory that only experience can be known. This dogmatic point of view is the empiricist's theory of knowledge in distinction to the empirical method for describing experience.

There is no necessary correlation between an empirical method, and an empiricist's theory of knowledge. An empirical method is simply a procedure for describing experience. Every description of experience, therefore, is an instance of the empirical method. But an empiricist's theory of knowledge is a proposition about what can be known. It is a dogmatic assertion that experience is known, and only experience is known, or knowable.

A confusion, therefore, between the empirical method as a procedure, and the empiricist's theory of knowledge, accounts for the dogmatism that when an empirical procedure is adopted, all that may be claimed as knowledge is confined to an empiricist's theory of knowledge. This, however, is not the case.

If there is a reality other than experience, one may designate an interpretation of it by symbols. But when symbols are used to designate interpretations of a reality other than language, the symbolic function of the interpretation itself must be taken into account. The symbolic function of language, in this case, would be a directing of attention beyond language itself, and so the nature of that to which it directs attention would not even be within the province of a language analyst to pass judgment upon. Analysts of language, of course, pass such judgments, but they pass these judgments not upon language, but upon what is symbolized in language.

To maintain that all symbols designate experience, and nothing other than experience, is simply dogmatic. To maintain, however, that some symbols designate experience, and other symbols designate interpretations of a reality which *may be* other than experience, is not dogmatic. To maintain, therefore, that some interpretations may be informed of such a reality other than experience is likewise free of the dogmatism from which radical empiricisms are not free.

Experiences may be interpreted from the point of view of more than one premise, and any one of these interpretations may constitute an internally consistent philosophy. But there will, of course, be different philosophies, because there are different interpretations of what may be known.

1. *A symbolic expression is not itself evidence for a reality other than experience.*

When by means of symbols an individual states an interpretation of a reality, the meaning of the symbols is for him his interpretation of the reality. A law in physical science, for example, is an interpretation of relationships which are believed to be properties of the physical world. As an interpretation, the law obviously is not a property of the physical world. It is a significantly stated interpretation; and an interpretation is an experience. But what is interpreted is not necessarily experience.

The assumption of every so-called realistic theory of knowledge is that there is a physical world whose nature is interpreted in the so-called "laws" of physical science. The belief, for example, that there is a correlation between the volume, pressure, and temperature of a gas is an interpretation of the properties of a physical reality. When stated as a generalization, this interpretation is a "scientific law".

According to a realistic theory of knowledge, the reality interpreted in the laws of physical science is external to experience. When its properties are interpreted, so that these properties inform interpretations, the interpretations are then said to be scientific knowledge.

Laws in science are assumed to have an interpretative function. As interpretations, they are experiences, but the reality which they are assumed to interpret may be other than experience. It is careless terminology, therefore, to speak of discovering a law: what is discovered are properties of a reality in some particular context, selected to substantiate an interpretation formulated as a law.

Every interpretation of a reality is to some extent other than the reality which is interpreted. The very fact that there is a distinction between an interpretation, and what is interpreted, is itself an acknowledgment that there are two entities. An interpretation of a reality is a claim to knowledge, and the reality of which knowledge is claimed is other than the knowledge claimed of it. This distinction, however, is commonly glossed over in accommodation to the presuppositions that what is known is experience.

Claims to knowledge indeed are experiences, but what makes one experience a claim to knowledge, and another experience not a claim to knowledge, is the very distinction itself between symbolic devices and what is symbolized. A symbol is always assumed to designate a reality which is other than the symbol. Such symbolic function, for example, is performed by the term "God" to designate a completely trustworthy reality. In contexts other than religious faith, the symbol "god" may designate anything. Hence, from the use of a symbol, nothing may be inferred about what is designated. More than a symbol must therefore be known before the significance of the symbol itself can be ascertained. What must be known is the context which is referred to when the symbol is used.

But the clarification of a context in which a symbol is used is an interpretation of the referent of the symbol. When Feuerbach, for example, uses the symbol "god", he refers to human experience. For him, the term "god" designates an individual's most respected ideal. Hence, when the symbol "god" is used as Feuerbach uses it, no individual could be designated an "atheist": whatever an individual values most is for him the significance designated by the symbol "god".

Feuerbach is entitled to state, as he does, the nature of the context to which he refers when he uses this particular term, but he certainly is not entitled to maintain that no other sense may be associated with the symbol than the sense he proposes. The term "God" may be used to designate a reality which is transcendent of experience, and this stipulation is as sound a procedure as is Feuerbach's. The symbol "God" is an arbitrary mark, but what is not arbitrary for an individual who believes that there is a divine reality transcendent of experience, and of the physical world, is the interpretation of this reality which is designated by the symbol "God". For the individual who believes that there is a divine reality other than the physical world, upon which the physical world is dependent, either for its origin, or for its purpose, or for both, the term "God" has a very special symbolic function.

When an individual believes that there is a divine reality other than human life, and other than the physical world, he uses the symbol "God" in a way that another does not use the symbol who does not believe that there is such a reality. From the use of a symbol, therefore, nothing may be inferred about the knowledge-value of the interpretation designated by the symbol. The significance of a symbol, however, can be ascertained by knowing which reality is designated by a symbol. The clarification of this symbolic function is thus an interpretation not only of a language-term, but also of a reality designated by a language-term.

When the symbolic function of language is presupposed, it is assumed that something is designated. What is designated may be interpretations; but interpretations may in turn be of realities other than symbols. This specific assumption is implied in the religious use of language symbols for designating a divine reality.

An interpretation may be designated by a symbol. But when a reality other than experience is assumed, an interpretation of its nature may also be designated by symbols. This latter symbolic procedure must, however, be distinguished from the procedure in which a symbol is used with a certain meaning, and from the meaning of the symbol, a reality other than the meaning is inferred. The latter procedure is the method of all who use the ontological argument. In the ontological argument, one begins with an idea of a reality, and from the idea of its existence, infers the existence of a reality other than the idea. Descartes, for one, believed that from his "idea of a thing more perfect than (him)self, it follows that this thing really exists." (2) The argument, of course, disregards the distinction between an idea of a reality other than experience, and the reality other than experience of which there is an idea. From the idea of a reality other than experience, nothing, however, may be inferred about the existence of a reality other than experience. But when it is assumed that there is such a reality, interpretations of its nature may be stated as knowledge-claims.

All who propose the ontological argument, therefore, reveal not only an ignorance of the nature of symbolism, but also what is far more tragic than any ignorance of academic distinctions: they disclose an arrogance which cannot appreciate the limitations of the resources for gaining knowledge of a reality other than experience.

Descartes, for example, assumed that he knew the nature of God, and because he was so confident that he had this information, he passed from *his* idea of God to the reality of God, as if there were an equivalence of the two. This passage is manifested in Descartes' affirmation that since he possesses "an idea of God (as a mind) . . . it must of necessity be admitted that it is . . . a thinking being, and that it possesses in itself . . . all the perfection *I* attribute to Deity." (3) Descartes presumes that what he believes to be the nature of God *is* the criterion itself by which knowledge-claims of the nature of God are to be evaluated. That this bigotry is the underlying mentality of all who use the ontological argument cannot be concealed. Whenever the ontological argument is proposed, knowledge-claims are confused with "knowledge of"; and interpretations of a divine reality are confused with the nature of the divine reality.

Descartes believed that God is "substance infinite, eternal, independent, all-knowing, all-powerful, by which everything that exists (was) . . . created." This idea of the divine reality is Descartes' interpretation, and when he uses the term "God", he means a reality such as is designated by this interpretation. But the reality which Descartes proposes to designate when he uses the symbol "God" is not his interpretation. Hence he does not begin his argument for the reality of God with his idea of a divine reality, and from the idea infers that there is a divine reality. He begins rather with a faith that there is a divine reality, and he regards his idea of God as an informed interpretation of the nature of the divine reality. But this judgment upon his interpretation is possible only because he assumes to know something of a reality other than his interpretation.

Many ideas have been proposed as interpretations of the divine reality: and yet, from ideas of the divine reality, nothing is known other than interpretations, unless the interpretations are informed. That some are informed is an assumption; and it is also an assumption about the existence of a reality other than interpretations. A disregard for this distinction between an interpretation, and a reality which is interpreted, however, accounts for Descartes' proposal to argue the reality of God from the idea of the reality of God. But since the idea of the reality of God is of something other than one's idea, the faith that there is a divine reality is already affirmed by the individual who proposes the ontological argument. This is obvious in the case of Anselm, from whom Descartes appropriated the argument, without, however, making one distinction which Anselm makes.

Anselm affirms the faith that "thou art a being than which nothing greater can be conceived." (4) This, however, is not the premise of an ontological argument: it is rather a statement of faith about the existence of a reality other than any interpretations. But ignoring the assumption of the existence of such a reality, Anselm proposed to argue that when there is the idea of God as "that, than which nothing greater can be conceived (then) there is no doubt that there exists a being, than which nothing greater can be conceived."

The confusion is obvious. Anselm believes that there is "a being than which nothing greater can be conceived", and with this faith, he proposes a statement about the nature of God. From this statement, he then assumes that he infers the existence of God in Whom he has his faith. But his faith is in the reality of God; an interpretation of Whom is the statement from which he presumes to demonstrate His existence.

That there is a divine reality, is a faith, and with this

faith, a religious individual interprets not only a reality other than his faith: he also interprets his faith. When the referent of faith is assumed to be a divine reality other than human experience, interpretations of this reality are themselves interpreted from the point of view of religious faith. Hence, a religious individual has a faith in the informed nature of interpretations of a divine reality, as well as in the divine reality he interprets.

2. *Religious faith may be assumed to interpret a reality other than experience.*

A religious individual does not assume that because there is a theological statement about the nature of a divine reality, there is a divine reality. He believes, rather, that there is a divine reality, and believing that something of its nature can be known in experience, he regards those interpretations of its nature to be informed which he believes interprets the nature of the divine reality.

Some point of view about a divine reality must, therefore, be regarded as informed before a theological statement can be evaluated as warranted. A religious individual who passes judgment upon a theological belief assumes that he knows something, not only about theology, but also about the divine reality. But when a theology consists of interpretations informed of the divine reality, it is informative not only of religious beliefs, but also of a reality other than religious beliefs. An evaluation of the merits of a theology, therefore, is not a matter purely of internal consistency, or of the logical use of language. It is also a matter of which beliefs are assumed to be informed of the nature of the divine reality.

9

FAITH IN KNOWLEDGE-CLAIMS

AN HYPOTHESIS is an assumption proposed to interpret some reality. When an hypothesis is stated, it is a proposition; and it may be said to be a true proposition when the interpretation stated in the hypothesis is informed of the nature of the reality which one endeavours to interpret.

An hypothesis, however, cannot even be evaluated as a probable interpretation of the nature of a reality unless something of the nature of the reality is presupposed. Thus, in evaluating the interpretative function of an hypothesis, an assumption is made in order to pass judgment upon another assumption. One is the hypothesis about the nature of the reality which is interpreted; the other is the assumption with which the hypothesis is evaluated. The notion, for example, that two volumes of the same text were produced by fingers running at random over the keys of a typewriter is an hypothesis about the production of two volumes. But the hypothesis is dismissed as fantastic because some other interpretation of the production of two identical copies is assumed as more probable.

Hypotheses differ in their credibility for an individual

because each individual assumes certain points of view, and these points of view he employs as criteria with which he evaluates other points of view. The particular point of view with which an interpretation of a reality is evaluated is an assumption about that reality. Hence, one hypothesis about a reality is evaluated only when another hypothesis is assumed as probably more informed of the nature of that reality. The rejection of an hypothesis, therefore, may reveal more about the confidence which an individual has in what he regards as knowledge than it discloses about the actual untenability of an hypothesis.

Every evaluation of the tenability, or untenability, of an hypothesis is a judgment from the point of view of another hypothesis. This holds even in such a simple situation as the explanation for the production of two copies of the same text. When one is already convinced of the tenability of one hypothesis, he believes that another which is contradictory of it is untenable. Thus what is believed to be the informative value of an hypothesis is determined by what is assumed to be the nature of the reality of which knowledge is claimed. This is circular, and yet, it is the point of view with which all claims to knowledge are assessed. In any evaluation of an interpretation of a reality, something of the nature of the reality itself must be assumed. But any assumption about its nature is itself an interpretation. Thus two interpretations are involved whenever claims to knowledge are assessed. In any evaluation of an interpretation, there is a contest for acceptance between one proposition and another. The proposition which is accepted by an individual is the one which is most credible to him. But the credibility of a proposition to an individual has no necessary correlation with its knowledge-value. It is only an expression of what an individual regards as knowledge, and expresses what he believes about the nature of a reality which he interprets.

If the only reality interpreted were an individual's own experience, an empiricist alone could account for knowledge-claims. They would be interpretations of experience. But if there is a reality other than experience which an individual endeavours to interpret, then he does not merely affirm interpretations of his experience. His interpretation is an experience, but the knowledge-value of his interpretation is a feature of informed experience.

Locke, for example, endeavoured to defend an empiricist's theory of knowledge, and therefore declared that "knowledge (is) nothing but the perception of the connection of an agreement or disagreement . . . of any of our ideas." (1) But this does not account for the features of knowledge-claims which are ventured about a reality believed to be other than experience. When a reality other than experience is interpreted, something other than experience is assumed to be known. Yet, what is known of its nature must always be in experience, and what is affirmed of its nature must always be a statement. The informative significance of an interpretation, however, is not a feature of language: language is simply an instrument developed to express interpretations.

What is assumed to be known is the reality interpreted: not just the interpretation. The interpretation is what is assumed to be known of the reality. If there is a reality whose properties are what an individual assumes they are, then an individual has knowledge of the reality. His possession of such knowledge, however, has nothing to do with the language he employs in articulating his knowledge. He may interpret a reality other than his experience, and he may be informed of its nature, even though he makes no effort to articulate the interpretation in a language form.

If, however, he articulates his interpretation, then the statement of his interpretation is the proposition whose knowledge-value may be estimated by others. But the estimate of its knowledge-value will always be from the point of view of an individual interpreting the reality. Thus the statement that the sun loses "mass at the rate of four million tons a second" (2) is an interpretation of a physical reality, something of whose nature is assumed to be known. Since this interpretation may have to be revised, it is regarded in science as an hypothesis. If it were assumed to be an interpretation which would not be revised, it would never be regarded as an hypothesis.

An hypothesis is an interpretation whose knowledge-value is subject to judgment, just as the hypothesis itself is subject to revision. This acknowledgment of its tentative character in the point of view which makes it an hypothesis. The caution, therefore, with which a claim to knowledge is regarded as an hypothesis is an admission that achieving knowledge is not merely a matter of venturing claims to knowledge. It is being informed of the nature of the reality of which one ventures an interpretation.

An interpretation is regarded as a knowledge-claim only when it is assumed that it is an informed interpretation. But this is an assumption, and it is as much of an act of faith as is the interpretation itself.

Every hypothesis in science is a claim to knowledge. It is an interpretation of a reality; but in proposing the interpretation, the admission is also implied that the interpretation may be insufficiently informed. An admission of its deficiency, however, in no way affects the informative value of the hypothesis: what one may think about an hypothesis has nothing to do with its knowledge-value. The hypothesis, for example, that the earth is a sphere was proposed by the Pythagoreans centuries before it was commonly accepted as a defensible interpretation. The tragedy that the human race should have remained so long in ignorance about the nature of the earth on which it lives has nothing to do with the soundness of the Pythagoreans' interpretation. The rejection of the interpretation proposed by the Pythagoreans is simply a commentary upon the tenacity with which individuals cling to what they believe to be knowledge. The tenacity, however, with which individuals cling to a belief has nothing to do with its knowledge-value. Even the number of individuals who cling to a belief has nothing whatsoever to do with its knowledge-value.

When an individual becomes aware of the moral responsibility imposed upon him in claiming to know something of a reality, he is already cautious about what he claims for his own interpretations. He regards them as subject to correction when he believes that more can be known of the nature of the reality which he proposes to interpret. Those, however, who have not achieved a moral maturity sufficient to recognize the obligations entailed in any claim to knowledge are aware of none of the responsibilities acknowledged by the individual who states his claims to knowledge as hypothesis. An hypothesis may be ventured with the strongest confidence that it is informed, and yet, an individual who knows something of the history of ideas also knows something of the folly of an unwillingness to learn more than one already assumes to know. The designation of a claim to

115

knowledge as an hypothesis is just this cautious evaluation of one's interpretation. It is an admission that an interpretation of a reality may be revised because more of its nature may be known than one assumes he already knows.

"Knowledge" must therefore be distinguished from "claims to knowledge". A claim to knowledge is knowledge when it is informed of the reality whose nature one proposes to interpret. But when an individual who proposes an interpretation does not also know that his interpretation is informed of the nature of the reality he proposes to interpret, he admits that his interpretation is an hypothesis. This admission is not a commentary on the knowledge-value of the interpretation. It is a commentary, rather, on the attitude of an individual toward his interpretation.

Earnest though an individual may be to know the nature of a reality, his earnestness as such has little merit unless his zeal is disciplined by the responsibilities which the "claim to knowledge" itself imposes. To claim that one knows a reality, imposes an obligation: it imposes the obligation to be informed. But the information of a reality is not a product of earnestness: earnestness is only a condition which motivates an individual to learn. Earnestness which is directed not upon learning, but upon maintaining that one already has learned all that he can know is a vice. It is a type of mentality which is not concerned to know all that might be known: it is concerned to restrict itself, and others, to what is assumed to be known.

The greatest zeal to know is compatible with classifying every claim to knowledge as an hypothesis, since what one believes is knowledge is after all an interpretation. The admission that an interpretation is an hypothesis is not a reservation in one's confidence in its truth. It is simply an acknowledgment that the quest for knowledge is a long search, and that more may be known than is already known. This caution does not diminish the zeal to know. It merely checks the arrogance of identifying one's beliefs about a reality, whether physical or divine, with the nature of the reality. This caution is the minimum condition in a search to know the nature of any reality as complex as the physical world, and as worthy to be known as the divine reality. To admit less than this caution is impudence.

Science is a search: so is religious life. A religious life is bent upon knowing something of the divine reality. It is not satisfied to know only what others believe about the divine reality. It may be interested in such beliefs as a help in its own search. But when others' beliefs become the only reality which one seeks to know, the objective of his knowledge-quest is not the divine reality. So likewise, when a science, as a body of beliefs, is the only reality which an individual desires to know, his desire is for something very different from the physical scientist's desire. A scientist seeks to know the physical reality. To gain such knowledge is his objective. But in his effort to attain this objective, he hesitates to classify his interpretations as knowledge. He therefore regards them as claims to knowledge, recognizing that a claim to knowledge is a classification of an interpretation; whereas knowledge is not. Knowledge is a property of an interpretation.

1. *Hypotheses in physical science are not interpretations of sensory experiences.*

Locke declares that "the idea of the sun . . . is

117

(nothing) but an aggregate of . . . several simple ideas—bright, hot, roundish, having a constant regular motion, at a certain distance from us." (3) The slightest comparison of this description of an idea of the sun with the knowledge-claims which are proposed in modern astronomy, however, reveals how great a disparity there is between an empirical description of an idea of a physical object, and the interpretation of the nature of the object, of which there may be some empirical information. The idea of the sun for a scientifically uninformed individual does include the vivid imagery of intense brightness, but it does not include an idea of temperature measured in thousands of degrees. The idea of a sun for such an individual may include the image of a circle, but it certainly does not include a notion of the dimensions of the sun as a body whose diameter is some 886,000 miles. The notion of the diameter of the sun in terms of hundreds of thousands of miles is a modern hypothesis, and from the data of visual experience alone, this hypothesis would never have entered the mind of man.

The idea of the sun for a primitive individual would indeed include a notion of movement, as Locke points out. But it would not include the idea of a movement of thousands of miles a day, any more than it would include the notion that the sun is the center around which the earth moves at a rate of more than a million miles a day. The idea of the sun even for a scientifically untrained individual includes a notion of a distance from the earth, but it certainly does not include the idea of a distance of some ninety-three million miles. A scientifically literate individual's idea of the sun today has few features in common with the idea of even the most learned of the ancient scientists. This fact should bring to anyone's attention that what is claimed in modern science as knowledge of the sun is not based on sensory data, and it is likewise not derived from an interpretation of sensory experience.

Very little of a modern scientist's idea of the nature of the sun is deduced from sensory data. An estimate, for example, of the temperature of the sun, and an estimate of the pressure of the gaseous state of the sun is an hypothesis about the nature of the sun. This hypothesis is not based upon sensory data, and it is not in any way derived from sensory experience. This fact becomes clear when the idea of the sun is analyzed. The idea of the sun for a scientist includes a belief that the sun is a parent of the planets, and this in turn includes a belief in the proximity of a wandering star which produced a pull upon the gaseous structure of the sun. The idea of the sun for a modern scientist likewise includes an interpretation of the nature of radiation: an interpretation of which in turn includes an hypothesis of the atom; and this in turn, of atomic components. Thus one cannot even begin to describe the properties of the physical sun without becoming involved in the most complex set of interpretations. This complex set of interpretations is the modern scientist's idea of the sun, and this idea has indeed little resemblance to the simple aggregate of sensory features as Locke proposed. Locke's attempt to describe the idea of the sun may take into account features which the idea of a primitive person may have of the sun, but it certainly does not describe the features of a scientifically literate individual's idea of the sun.

No one would think of accounting for the discovery of the planet Neptune by the method of Locke's description of ideas. Before Neptune was photographed, the idea of Neptune was an hypothesis. The hypothesis of Neptune's existence affirmed the faith that there must be an unobserved planet to account for the observed movements of the planet Uranus. But the movements of Uranus might have been observed by astronomers without proposing the existence of Neptune. Any number of explanations might have been proposed. Yet, when an astronomer observes certain movements, the movements are for him evidence of a causal factor which is interpreted according to the points of view formulated by Kepler and Newton, to mention only two of any number of others whose interpretations of the physical world enter into any interpretation proposed by an informed scientist today.

It is, however, impossible to describe the full meaning of an idea of the movements of Uranus without becoming involved in the entire physics of the solar system, and this in turn involving an interpretation of the solar system in the galactic setting, and this in turn in the setting of other comparable systems. All of this is included in the idea of the movements of Uranus. When the complex nature of the movements of Uranus is analyzed, the hypothesis of a planet having a particular location in the solar system is already formulated. Hence, the specific direction stipulated in this hypothesis itself directed astronomers to photograph the planet.

This discovery of Neptune cannot be accounted for by any empiricist's analysis of the character of Locke's or Hume's. The discovery of Neptune was not brought about by an analysis of sensory data, or by a reflection upon sensory data. The sensory data involved in the discovery of the planet were interpreted from the point of view of the hypothesis of a planet in the gravitational field of Uranus. After a complex calculation of the movements of Uranus, the mass and distance of Neptune were estimated, even before Neptune was photographed. By means of these estimates, a photograph of Neptune was made possible. But no one would propose that a description of the photographic figure had anything to do with securing the photograph of Neptune.

The same criticism of an empiricist's theory of scientific methodology must be offered in an analysis of the method of any other physical science. When, for example, one looks at water, he may well describe his experiences, but any such description of his experiences in terms of sensory data in no way bears any resemblance whatsoever to all that is claimed as knowledge of the structure of water. A scientific interpretation of the nature of water *involves an idea of molecular structure*. The idea of a molecule includes the idea of an atom; the idea of an atom in turn includes the idea of the electron, and so on.

Whatever basis there is upon which the molecular and atomic structure of a physical object rests, it is not sensory data. With the hypothesis of molecular and atomic structures, rather, sensory data have a significance which they would not have without these hypotheses. But the order of significance is not from sensory data to scientific hypotheses: it is from hypotheses to an interpretation of sensory data. This fact is obvious in analyzing the concept of the mass of a helium atom.

An estimate of the mass of the helium atom and of the hydrogen atom necessitates the hypothesis of radiation. The interpretation of the mass of the helium atom as four times the mass of the hydrogen atom follows from the assumption that four hydrogen atoms combine to form one helium atom. But although the mass of the helium atom is designated as four, the mass of the hydrogen atom may not be inferred as one, since it is found to be more than one. The difference between the mass of a hydrogen atom as 1.008, and the mass of the helium atom as 4, is, however, accounted for by the hypothesis of radiation. According to this hypothesis, energy is lost by radiation when four hydrogen atoms combine to form one helium atom.

With this hypothesis, which is proposed to account for a basic phenomenon in chemistry, an idea is gained about the possible nature of radiation in the stars. Thus the same hypothesis which is proposed to account for the discrepancy of atomic weights of two elements with which chemists are acquainted in the laboratory, is also proposed to account for stellar radiation. Such an extension of the scope of an hypothesis from a chemist's laboratory to the interior of the stars rests upon many assumptions. If modern scientists still believed as Aristotle, and most pre-Copernican scientists, that there is a fundamental difference in the nature of the heavenly bodies and the earth, this extension of the hypothesis of radiation would never have been ventured. But what is done with one hypothesis is conditioned by what is believed about the field of its application. The scope of application of an hypothesis, however, is itself an hypothesis. The same type of radiation which is proposed to account for one of the elements in the composition of the earth is proposed to account for the radiation of the sun, and because our sun is a star, this radiation is also proposed to interpret the nature of the stars. But this extension from the radiation of the sun to the radiation of the stars rests upon the hypothesis of the common physical composition of sun and stars. Thus with this assumption, the composition of the earth becomes linked with the composition of the remotest star. But the composition of the remotest star is not something observed. It is an interpretation implied in the hypothesis of the common character of all physical bodies.

Confined to the range of senses, one must ask how the notion of an expanding universe would ever arise. Even if the notion of an expansion of the apparent vault of the sky were conceived, what possible correlation would there be between the restricted dimensions associated with interpretations of sensory data, and the incredible estimates of a universe doubling in size every 1,300 million years or so? (4)

The idea of the expanding universe, like the idea of the common character of radiation of terrestrial and stellar bodies, is an hypothesis, or a venture of faith. It is an interpretation of a reality which is believed to have certain properties. But these properties are not inferred from features of sensory data. These interpretations are rather assumptions about the nature of physical reality, whether it be the universe, or an atom.

Neither the universe nor the atom are observable. Certain data, however, within the limited scope of observations are interpreted from the point of view that there is a universe of vast dimensions, and that there is an atomic structure of infinitesimal dimensions. But the very vast, and the very small, are not observed. Their structures are interpreted, and the interpretations of their structures are hypotheses.

Hypothetical constructions may account for data which is observed, but many, or most, of the hypotheses in theoretical science are not formulated to make sensory data credible to an individual. The motive in scientific research is not to account for sensory data: it is to become informed of the nature of the realities in relation to which an individual assumes he has some experience.

Every primitive person who survived very long observed his environment carefully enough to get out of the way of falling stones, or to get out of the way of rocks hurled by an enemy. But no primitive person ever observed kinetic energy. It is only a mind curious enough to account for bodies which are believed to be observed that proposes the hypothesis of energy, and proposes that the energy of a falling body is potential in the body before it falls. But no one, whether a primitive, or a contemporary scientist, observes potential energy. The concept of energy is an hypothesis which includes the notion of potential energy transformable into kinetic energy. The notion that there is an energy before it is converted is an interpretation of a property of a physical body which is believed to be observed.

All hypotheses in theoretical science are normative ideas, or ideals. The notion of a simple pendulum, for example, is a normative idea which is not derived from any number of observations of particular physical phenomena. It is an hypothesis about particular phenomena in the physical world. The notion of the average velocity of a molecule is another such ideal. It is not a descriptive analysis of any observable data. Observable data do not even enter into the idea of the average velocity of a molecule. Yet, this idea is a part of physical science. No single molecule could be observed, any more than could the movements of a single molecule be measured. Yet, the idea of the average velocity of a molecule is a magnitude which is employed in interpreting the pressure and density of actual gases.

Certain sensory data may be the manifestations in experience of a physical gas existing as a reality other than experience, but from such data nothing would be inferred about an ideal gas, or about an ideal molecule of a gas. One need not press the analysis of scientific ideas very far to see that they are not descriptions of sensory data; and that they are not interpretations of experience. They are interpretations of realities other than experience, and with such interpretations, certain data of experience are in turn accounted for, or interpreted.

Hypotheses in physical science are methodological simplifications. The idea of an ideal gas, for example, interprets a less complex entity than an actual gas, since an actual gas is affected by all the factors in its physical context. Newton's first law, likewise, states relations which are less complicated than the actual relations in the physical world. In the ideal formulated by Newton, a physical body would continue in a path of movement without deflection if not acted upon by another body. That there is no body in the entire physical universe which is free of the influence of other bodies is obvious to anyone who understands the meaning of gravitation. Gravitation is the action of one body upon another, and yet, the excessive simplification in Newton's first law makes it possible to calculate the amount of gravitational attraction upon a body in relation to other bodies. The first law of Newton is an abstraction in the sense that properties of a body are abstracted from all actual bodies, and are conceived as properties of an ideal body. The ideal body, however, is not an interpretation of any particular actual body; yet, a particular actual body may be interpreted from the point of view of the nature of the ideal body.

From particular data which are observed, it is obvious that nothing would ever be mentioned about the average velocity of a molecule in an ideal gas, any more than anything would be mentioned about the correlation of pressure, temperature, and volume of gases. But there is enough curiosity peculiar to some minds to want to know the nature of a physical reality which is assumed to be related to the data observed.

Interpretations of this physical reality constitute physical science as a system of concepts about the physical world. These concepts are not hypotheses about experience. But with these concepts, some of the data of experience are accounted for. The order cannot, however, be reversed. Systems of science are not derived from the data of sensory experiences: it is the mind which correlates features of sensory data with properties of the physical world. But the correlation rests upon the assumption that there is a physical world whose properties account for some of the features of sensory experience.

This assumption, however, is the basic act of faith in a theory about the knowledge-value of science. Unless something were assumed to be known of the nature of a reality other than experience, no effort would ever be made to assess the warrant for the knowledge-claims in physical science.

One cannot go far in any theory of knowledge, or in any analysis of the knowledge-claims in physical science, without realizing how very inadequate is Hume's premise that all ideas are faint images of sensory "impressions". When sensory experiences are regarded as the basis for ideas, an empiricist simply cannot account for some ideas. The idea, for example, that there is an identity of experiences cannot be accounted for in terms of sensory

126

experiences. Identity is a concept: it is an idea with which particular experiences may be classified. But the classification of particular experiences as identical is an operation upon experiences which cannot itself be accounted for in terms of particular experiences.

Particular data are classified as instances of a class only when the notion of a class is employed, and this notion cannot be derived from particulars. In the classification of particulars, more than particular sensory data are involved: the particular data are interpreted from the point of view of a class. It is just this type of interpretation of particular data as instances of a class, however, which constitutes one of the difficulties in pressing the empiricist's analysis of *all* ideas, and so *all* knowledge-claims, as derivations from sensory data.

2. *Hypotheses are statements of faith.*

An hypothesis is a belief about something whose nature one endeavours to understand, and its function in physical science is as clear an instance of an act of faith as one can find. An hypothesis is ventured by an individual who regards it as a warranted interpretation of some property of the physical world; but he ventures it as an assumption whose warrantability is not known. Its warrant, however, is assumed. If it were not assumed, it would not even be proposed as an interpretation. An individual's uncertainty, however, in estimating the warrant for an hypothesis is not a measure of the probability of its soundness: it is simply an expression of the individual's hesitancy to assert that the hypothesis is warranted.

One ventures an interpretation of a reality even when he is not able to justify the interpretation he affirms. This

127

very inability to accompany an interpretation with the credentials for its warrant is just the nature of an hypothesis. An hypothesis, however, which is regarded by an individual as an interpretation of a reality, of whose nature he assumes he knows less than he might know, is an expression of faith. It expresses a faith that his interpretation is warranted, although he does not possess certification for the warrant of his interpretation.

An hypothesis is an interpretation which is ventured at the same time that one hesitates to claim that it is an informed interpretation, and yet, one proposes the interpretation because he assumes it is informed. There is nothing contradictory in this. It is the characteristic of all honest interpretation. An honest individual always proposes the most informed statements he can about the nature of a reality he attempts to interpret; and yet, when he is aware of the difficulty of attaining knowledge, he is also hesitant to assume that every belief he assumes to be warranted is actually warranted. Thus there is a very great difference in believing that one's interpretations are claims to knowledge, and in believing that one's interpretations qualify as knowledge.

It is one thing to know one's interpretations: it is quite another thing to know that one's interpretations of a reality are informed of the nature of the reality interpreted. Yet, the presumption that some interpretations are informed is the presupposition underlying all science. Interpretations are classified as warranted points of view because an assumption is made about their informative-value. But the informative-value of propositions in science is their adequacy to state interpretations which are warranted. They are warranted when they are informed. Yet, the whole objective of scientific study is to know which interpretations are warranted.

Science is an endless quest for the very reason that the warrant for interpretations will always remain a challenge. So long as there are interpretations of the nature of a reality other than an individual's own point of view, so long will an individual who is in an earnest search of knowledge be aware that his interpretation is not a final judgment. There is still another judgment: it is a judgment upon the warrant for his interpretation.

This distinction constitutes the basis for a differentiation in the objects of which a probability-estimate is made. One estimates the probability that his interpretation is warranted. Yet, the estimate of this probability is not necessarily an expression of its informative-value. The evaluation of an interpretation in terms of the probability that it is informed is other than the informative-value of the interpretation. An interpretation is informed when the nature of a reality is analyzed correctly in the interpretation. But an individual who proposes an interpretation of a reality may not even be aware of the accuracy with which he actually does interpret the reality. Hence, he may be unable accurately to evaluate the probable knowledge-value of his interpretation.

This is not a contradiction: it is an acknowledgment that a claim to knowledge of a reality may be made even though an individual may not know that he knows the nature of the reality. The warrant for an interpretation is assumed: otherwise it would not be proposed as a serious point of view.

Interpretations of the physical world constitute science. Whether these interpretations are warranted claims to knowledge, however, is a problem which no scientist at any time in the history of science can pass judgment upon with "warranted" certainty. Yet, every scientist regards claims to knowledge as warranted, and these claims to knowledge are a scientist's equipment in ascertaining their warrant. Thus there is a circular feature in all scientific research. An interpretation is assumed to be warranted, and yet, the justification for research is to ascertain the warrant for interpretations.

Every claim to knowledge is an expression of faith. It is a venture to believe something about the warrant for one's point of view. Data are selected as confirming evidence for a point of view only when the data are assumed to be relevant. But this assumption is itself a judgment about realities other than the point of view. An individual may very well be aware of what his point of view is, and yet he would have to make assumptions about other realities if he were to subject the point of view to "empirical" testing. Empirical testing of a point of view is confronting a point of view with data which are not included in the point of view.

The selection of such data rests upon the assumption of the relevance of data to confirm an interpretation. But the circular character of this testing is obvious: data are interpreted as evidence for a point of view, and therefore are selected as confirming it. But the selection is an interpretation of data from the point of view of what one is looking for. Only the most superficial of mentality could gloss over this profound problem with which an individual is confronted who earnestly endeavours to evaluate the warrant for selecting data as evidence to confirm his point of view. What is regarded as confirmatory evidence is interpreted as relevant: but a confidence in the defensibility of an interpretation may itself make an individual assume that data are relevant. This influence of a point of view upon the selection of evidence for "empirically testing" the point of view itself is indeed a very sobering fact. It makes one realize that claims to "objective verification", or "objectivity" are indefensible boasts.

No one aware of the offense of the boast would propose that some points of view are not objective. To know this much would indeed be possessing vast information, but one would be totally uninformed about the nature of knowing to claim that his points of view are objective in the sense that he knows they are informed of the nature of a reality which he proposes to interpret.

Locke declares that "he who would not deceive himself ought to build his hypothesis on matter of fact . . . and not presume on matter of fact because of his hypothesis." (5) This prescription is certainly a recommendation it would be desirable to follow, but whose requirement is more of a fictional ideal than most advocates of the "empirical" method might care to admit. What are regarded as "facts" are interpreted data, and when data are interpreted as "facts", a faith is already affirmed that there is a reality other than an individual's present interpretation.

A religious individual does not claim to know only his interpretation when he believes there is a divine reality transcendent of human life, into whose purpose the history of the world somehow enters. When St. Augustine declares that "our souls may from their weariness arise toward Thee, leaning on those things which Thou has created, and passing on to Thyself" (6), he assumes that there is a divine reality other than human life, and other than the physical world. But this interpretation of a physical world as evidence for a reality other than the world itself is possible only for an individual who ventures the faith that there is a reality other than the physical world.

A religious interpretation of the world in terms of its expression of a divine purpose involves the same type of faith as is involved in interpreting sensory data as evidence of a physical reality. In both interpretations, an individual assumes that there is a reality other than experience. The religious individual, who like St. Thomas, argues that "our intellect knows God from creatures" (7), must first assume that there is a divine reality which is the Creator. Without this faith, no living thing would ever be interpreted as an instance of the creative nature of God. But the function of faith in interpreting the physical world as evidence for the creative activity of God is the same function which faith performs in interpreting sensory data as evidence for a physical reality. (8)

Religious faith is a point of view with which some experiences are interpreted. This is circular, of course, just as is the interpretation of sensory data as evidence for properties of a physical world. The properties of a physical world are assumed to be correlated with features of experience, and from the data of experience, knowledge is claimed of the properties of a reality which is other than experience. This procedure in the empirical method of science is the same procedure which underlies the interpretations which a religious individual makes.

When St. Thomas maintains that "our knowledge of God is derived from the perfections which flow from Him to creatures" (9), he affirms a faith. This is a religious interpretation of life. It regards life as significant in a plan, the working out of which is a divine purpose; and without this faith, life would not be interpreted in terms of its reference to a reality transcendent of the physical world. But with this faith, a significance is found in life which could not be found without this faith. If this is a reading of significance into reality, then it is the same process which underlies every claim in physical science to an "empirical" knowledge of a physical reality. (10)

10

THE CRITERION OF RELIGIOUS KNOWLEDGE-CLAIMS

AN INDIVIDUAL who seriously reflects upon beliefs which are regarded as claims to knowledge raises the question of the warrant for knowledge-claims. This question expresses an awareness of the need for criteria by which the warrant for knowledge-claims may be evaluated.

An individual who believes that religious life is a condition for attaining knowledge of a divine reality becomes aware sooner or later that claims to knowledge of the divine reality must be confronted by a criterion for their warrant. The criterion by which an individual evaluates the warrant for a claim to knowledge of the divine reality is what he believes to be a true interpretation of the divine reality. The religious quest to know the divine reality is itself a search for a criterion by which one may evaluate beliefs about the divine reality.

The faith of an earnest religious individual is the conviction that there is a reality other than human life, and other than the physical world, a knowledge of which would constitute a completely dependable guidance for life. Thus religious faith itself defines a standard by which religious life must evaluate claims to a knowledge of divine reality. This standard is complete dependability for human life. Where this is found, there alone one may believe he has discovered the divine reality. And every claim to a knowledge of the divine reality which does not formulate a completely trustworthy pattern of life for all men must be rejected as an interpretation of the divine reality. The conviction that there is one, and only one, completely trustworthy reality upon which human life may always depend is religious faith. According to this faith, when a dependable way of life for all men is not known, the divine reality is not known. And because what is a completely dependable way of life is a knowledge of the divine reality, religious faith affirms that one knows the Way, when he has such dependable knowledge. Religious faith is the confidence that there is a Way which may be known which "leadeth unto life", and the supreme purpose in life is to attain a knowledge of it that one may live enlightened by it. This is the pasturage for the soul of which Plato speaks. (1)

What is completely dependable for human life according to the criterion affirmed in religious life is the divine reality. But the faith that there is such a completely dependable reality whose nature man can know is not itself an adequate norm for ascertaining the truth-character of religious faith. Since a faith must be judged by a norm other than itself, so likewise must interpretations of faith be evaluated by criteria other than interpretations of faith. This becomes apparent when one recalls how some of the learned Pharisees declared that Jesus "is not of God, because he keepeth not the Sabbath day". (2) The criterion by which the Pharisees evaluated the authority of Jesus was institutional: it was the meaning which the Sabbath had in the religious culture of the day. Hence when Jesus challenged the institutional interpretation of the observances of the Sabbath, the Sabbath as interpreted by the institution was itself challenged as the criterion of religious life. This incident illustrates the fundamental problem confronting religious life when religious interpretations become the criteria of what is warranted religious faith. When a belief which is endorsed by an institution becomes the criterion by which all religious faith is measured, the religious institution may itself become an obstacle in man's religious quest.

Religious life is a striving to know the divine reality as the guidance for one's life; it is not a search to know what is believed in a religious institution about the divine reality, unless an institution does actually make available for men true interpretations of the divine reality. But evaluating the truth-character of institutional claims to a knowledge of the divine reality is just one responsibility of an earnest religious life.

An institution endorses a belief as an authorized canon in order to preserve its own identity as a religious institution, since it is only through an historical continuity of religious belief that there is also an historical continuity of a religious institution. And conversely, it is only through a religious institution that there is a continuity of a particular system of religious beliefs. But the system of beliefs canonized by a religious institution must, according to religious faith, be evaluated by a criterion of what religious life ought to believe about the divine reality. Hence an institutional canon as a "determination of revealed truth" is, as Brunner points out, "as perilous as it is necessary". (3) It is necessary, for only as there is a criterion of religious belief can one select from among divergent beliefs the ones which he regards as true. But the fundamental problem in religious life is not to ascertain what is consonant with the canon of a religious institution. The real problem is to ascertain what the canon itself ought to be.

An institution is a product of human effort, and therefore it is always subject to the limitations of human culture. It is from the unworthy features of such limitations, however, that the religious quest itself seeks to liberate human life. Consequently, if the very goal of the religious search is not to be defeated by an institution developed to assist in the search, institutions must themselves be subjected to earnest scrutiny.

An institutional canon of belief constitutes a grave problem for earnest religious life, and for this reason, Brunner maintains that "Bible faith will have to prove its vitality by its power of maintaining faith in the canon simultaneously with the necessity for Biblical criticism." (4) But this, however, is the problem: what shall constitute the norm for the criticism of the sacred scriptures canonized in religious tradition? Religious tradition is crystallized in its scriptures. But if a product of religious tradition is to constitute the final norm of religious faith, then religious faith will be constricted in its search to what is believed to be a knowledge of the divine reality. If an institution, however, is to be effective in directing men's lives to know the divine reality, it must itself be measured by the criterion of a true interpretation of the divine reality. If the end of the religious institution is to orient life to the divine reality, the criterion by which its instrumentality must be measured can, therefore, be nothing less than the divine reality itself.

A knowledge of the divine reality as the objective of

the religious quest thus imposes upon religious life a single norm. But there is no such singularity of norm even in the Bible. The Sermon on the Mount is not on the same level of significance as are some of the practical suggestions given by Jesus to His disciples. In view of the fact that the disciples were sent "forth as sheep in the midst of wolves", Jesus is credited with giving the practical advice that they should be "as wise as serpents (as well as) harmless as doves." (5) This counsel, however, is a part of the same canon as is the Sermon on the Mount. A biblical canon therefore which includes statements of belief as diverse as practical prudence and the Sermon on the Mount is not itself one norm.

The biblical canon is itself an institution's judgment upon the warrant for claims to a knowledge of the divine reality. Luther's antagonism to the Epistle of James, for example, was a consequence of his concept of what constitutes warranted religious belief. But surely his belief no more than some of the beliefs in the institution he sought to reform constitutes the final norm by which the warrant for beliefs of religious faith are to be judged.

It is begging the question to argue that the Bible "is the word precisely in virtue of the fact that it reserves to faith the verdict that it is the word of God." (6) This is circular, and constitutes nothing more than a subjective criterion for what is accepted as the word of God. The problem, however, of which an earnest religious life is actually aware is the need to have a knowledge of the divine reality in order to be freed from the misinterpretations of individuals and institutions. The circular definition of an institutional canon, therefore, in terms of the canon itself is not acceptable to an individual who seeks to know the divine reality, rather than what has been thought about it.

A scriptural canon is a product of applying a criterion in the selection of writings to be included in an authorized scripture. The criterion by which such selection is made is obviously not exempt from the errors of human judgment since it is itself a product of human judgment. A fact which cannot be ignored is that in the formation of the Old and New Testaments, a vast amount of writing was rejected as apocryphal which some individuals believed was revealed to men by God. Yet such rejection of writings, claimed to be true interpretations of the divine reality, implies that one criterion was used to contest another criterion.

The criterion by which the scriptural canon was formulated is a proximate criterion, since it is what was believed at the time of its formation to be a true interpretation of the divine reality. Religious faith, however, is the conviction that the divine reality is itself the norm by which all interpretations of its nature must be ultimately judged. Thus religious faith proposes the norm of the divine reality as the criterion of the truth-character of religious beliefs, and so affirms that a scripture is an authentic norm only insofar as its interpretations of the divine reality are informed of the nature of the divine reality.

But when a canon of a religious institution becomes the norm for the truth-character of all beliefs in science, as well as in religion, the same difficulty is involved for science as is involved for religious life itself. But St. Thomas Aquinas stipulates such a precarious norm when he declares that "whatsoever is found in the other sciences contrary to the truth of this science (i. e., sacred doctrine) must be condemned as false." (7) If, to be sure, certain theological concepts were so completely informed of all reality that no other interpretation could be more informed, then the dogma of Aquinas would be warranted.

It would, however, be the completest form of presumption to maintain that some institutions possess so completely the knowledge of the divine reality that never again in history will there be a fuller knowledge of its nature. This is not a religious testimony: it is rather the expression of a bigotry which is not humbled by religious faith. The conviction of religious faith is that through striving for a knowledge of the divine reality, more can be known than could be known without the earnest search; and when in the process of striving, more conditions are fulfilled for knowing its nature, more of its nature will be known.

This does not mean that scriptural teachings are not normative for Christian living: it means only that an individual Christian is making a vast presumption when he believes that *his* understanding of the scriptural record is so adequate that it cannot be improved. Even though the teachings of Jesus are normative for Christian living, this can not be construed to mean that any individual's understanding of their meaning is correspondingly normative, or even that an institution's interpretation is the final norm of what interpretations should be. Although the teachings of Jesus do constitute the norm for Christian belief, the problem nevertheless remains for every Christian to prepare himself so that his understanding of the teachings may be the meaning intended by Jesus. The norm, in turn, which Jesus proposed for the authenticity of his teachings about the will of God is the will of God. Hence, the recorded teachings of Jesus constitute a proximate norm, and even if an individual understood the teachings as recorded, the fact would still remain that those who recorded the teachings of Jesus, and those who translated them, did so within the limits of language, and within the limits of their understanding. Or as John Locke declares, "God does not unmake the man when he makes the prophet."

Although the scriptural teachings of Jesus constitute, as Brunner points out, "the main subject of Christian doctrine" (8), the fact still remains that Christian doctrine can be no more informed about the divine reality than are interpretations recorded in the Scripture. Since the teachings of Jesus are interpreted by men, the statements constituting Scripture are necessarily conditioned by human factors. Hence the conviction that the Bible "is the word of God" must itself be clarified, for it is ambiguous. It may mean two vastly different things. It may mean that the Bible as a human possession is an exhaustive analysis of the nature of the divine reality. But it surely cannot mean this. This would be a presumption for anyone to believe that man had as an historical possession, a complete knowledge of all that should be known of the divine reality and its significance for human life. It may also mean that in the Bible there may be found an authentic interpretation of the divine reality. According to this interpretation, although the formation of the Bible is conditioned by human understanding, nevertheless, what is informed of the divine nature in the Scripture is a true interpretation of its nature.

The Bible may be one source for a knowledge of God, but it is inconsistent with teachings in the Bible to maintain that the Bible is the only source for such knowledge. St. Paul specifically declares that "the invisible things of Him from the creation of the world are clearly seen . . . even His eternal power and Godhead," (9) and this knowledge of God is not derived from the Scripture. The Psalms, likewise, as part of the Scripture, maintain that there is a source for knowing the nature of God which is not confined to the Scripture. Hence the dogma that the Scripture are the one and only source for a knowledge of God, as well as the criterion for all knowledge-claims of the nature of God, is inconsistent with the Scripture itself.

Brunner declares that "the Scriptures do not figure in Christian theology . . . as the expression of faith, but as the ground and norm of faith." (10) But, as has been pointed out, a religiously motivated use of the Scripture to enable one to know the divine reality must itself be submitted to a norm which is other than the Scripture. Scripture is a warranted norm for evaluating religious beliefs only if the scriptural interpretation of the nature of God is informed of the nature of God, and then the problem always confronts one whether *his* interpretation of the Scripture is what is the intended significance of the Scripture.

The norm of religious knowledge is not man's understanding, or reason, for, as Brunner points out, "we measure reason and indeed all knowledge by God's word in Scripture." (11) This norm, however, can mean only one thing. It is not Scripture as a canon, for this is an institutional product. It is rather the nature of God as informs interpretations in Scripture. Hence the criterion for the truth-character of scriptural interpretations of the divine nature is not Scripture. It is the nature of God.

It is, therefore, indefensible to maintain, as Brunner

NOTES

Chapter One

1. Frege, G., "On Sense and Nominatum", *Readings in Philosophical Analysis*, ed. H. Feigl, W. Sellars, p. 91ff. Appleton-Century-Crofts, Inc., N. Y. 1949.
2. Ogden, C. K., Richards, I. A., *The Meaning of Meaning*, p. 88. Harcourt, Brace and Co., N. Y., 1948, revised.
3. Bertrand Russell points out that "there are an infinite number of interpretations satisfying these conditions, but there is only one among them which also satisfies empirical statements of enumeration, such as 'I have 10 fingers'. In this case, therefore, there is one interpretation which is very much more convenient than any of the others." *Human Knowledge*, p. 241, Simon and Schuster, Inc., N. Y., 1948.
4. Pap, A., *Elements of Analytic Philosophy*, p. 366, Macmillan Co., N. Y., 1949.
5. Schlick, M., "Causality in Everyday Life and in Recent Science", *Readings in Philosophical Analysis*, p. 516.
6. Russell says that "the first stage for the logician is to substitute: 'Whatever x may be, either x is not a dog or x barks.' But since dogs only bark sometimes, you have to substitute for 'x barks' the statement 'there is a time that x barks' . . . In the end you will arrive at a statement of enormous length, not only about dogs but about everything in the universe." *Op. cit.*, p. 431.
7. Whitehead, A. N., *Symbolism, Its Meanings and Effect*, p. 61, Macmillan Co., N. Y., 1927.
8. *The Meaning of Meaning*, p. 40.
9. *Confessions*, Bk. XII.

Chapter Two

1. Nagel, E., "Logic Without Ontology", *Readings in Philosophical Analysis*, p. 197 (Hereafter referred to as *Readings*)
2. Ogden and Richards, *op. cit.*, p. 121.
3. *Metaphysics* 992a.
4. *Republic* VII, 531 D.
5. Sellars, W., "Realism and the New Way of Words," *Readings*, p. 439.
6. *Prolegomena to any Future Metaphysics*, p. 85, Open Court, Chicago, 1933.

NOTES

Chapter Three

1. *Prolegomena to any Future Metaphysics*, p. 85.
2. *Ibid*, p. 49.
3. *Ibid*, p. 34.
4. *Ibid*, p. 79-80.
5. *Ibid*, p. 42.
6. *Ibid*, p. 35 (underlining mine).
7. *Ibid*, p. 78.
8. *Ibid*, p. 77.
9. *Ibid*, p. 72 (underlining mine).
10. *Ibid*, p. 84.
11. *Ibid*, p. 83.
12. *Ibid*, p. 13.
13. *Ibid*, p. 143 (underlining mine).
14. *Ibid*, p. 144.
15. *Ibid*, p. 134.
16. *Ibid*, p. 109.
17. *Ibid*, p. 109.
18. *Ibid*, p. 134.
19. *Ibid*, p. 48.
20. *Ibid*, p. 70.
21. *Ibid*, p. 5.
22. *Ibid*, p. 28.
23. *An Enquiry Concerning Human Understanding*, p. 84-85, Open Court, Chicago, 1924.
24. *Ibid*, p. 33.
25. *Ibid*, p. 43.
26. *Physics and Philosophy*, p. 16, Cambridge University Press, N. Y., 1943.
27. *Ibid*, p. 79.
28. *Ibid*, p. 7.
29. *Ibid*, p. 49.
30. *Ibid*, p. 80.
31. *Ibid*, p. 8.
32. *Ibid*, p. 29.
33. *Ibid*, p. 8.
34. *Ibid*, p. 15.
35. *Ibid*, p. 15.
36. *Ibid*, p. 11.

Chapter Four

1. *The Idea of the Holy*, p. 7, Ninth Impression, Oxford University Press, London, 1943, Trans. J. W. Harvey.
2. *Ibid*, p. 15.
3. *Ibid*, p. 16.
4. *Ibid*, p. 31.

5. *Ibid*, p. 128.
6. *Ibid*, p. 97.
7. *Ibid*, p. 52.
8. *Ibid*, p. 52.
9. *Ibid*, p. 20.
10. *Ibid*, p. 32.
11. *Ibid*, p. 32.
12. *Ibid*, p. 30.
13. *Ibid*, p. 19.
14. *Concerning Divine Names*, Ch. III, Sec. 7, p. 39ff, Trans. J. Parker.
15. Otto, R., *op. cit.*, p. 188, Appendix 1.
16. *Ibid*, p. 197, Appendix II (underlining mine).
17. *Ibid*, p. 131.
18. *Ibid*, "Forward", (underlining mine).
19. Otto declares that "the element of 'energy' reappears in Fichte's specu- lations on the Absolute as the gigantic, never-resting, active World- stress, and in Schopenhauer's daemonic 'Will' . . . both these writers are guilty of the same error that is already found in Myth; they transfer 'natural' attributes, which ought only to be used as 'ideograms' for what is itself properly beyond utterance, to the non-rational as real qualifica- tions of it, and they mistake symbolic expressions of feelings for adequate concepts upon which a 'scientific' structure of knowledge may be based." p. 24.
20. *Prolegomena*, p. 74.
21. *Confessions of St. Augustine*, Bk. VII.

Chapter Five

1. Pap, A., *op. cit.*, p. 324, footnote 18.
2. Ogden and Richards, *op. cit.*, p. 132.
3. *Ibid*, p. 131.
4. *Leviathan*, Ch. xxxi.
5. Pap, A., *op cit.*, p. 42, stating the position of Ayer and Carnap.
6. *Op. cit.*, p. 158; p. 235.
7. *Ibid*, p. 239.
8. Feigl, H., "Logical Empiricism", *Readings*, p. 7. But, as W. M. Urban points out, although "the language of religion is . . . evocative . . . it is also invocative. It evokes feelings but it also invokes objects. Invocation of . . . the Godhead itself, is of the very essence of religion, and distin- guishes its language from that of poetry." *Language and Reality*, p. 573. Macmillan, N. Y., 1939.
9. As Professor Urban declares, "to call God 'father almighty' and 'maker of heaven and earth' is to use dramatic language, but in this language are rendered relations which are metaphysical in character. The Christian creed is said to suffer from the injection of Greek metaphysics, but if it did not use a metaphysical language it would be *mere* poetry." *Op. cit.*, p. 575.

NOTES

10. "It is of course," as Professor H. R. Mackintosh says, a "question whether the . . . limitation of knowledge as such to the sense-word can be admitted as anything more than an arbitrary feat of definition." *Types of Modern Theology,* p. 21, Scribner's, N. Y., 1947.

11. Feigl, H., "Logical Empiricism", *op. cit.,* p. 12.

12. Pap, A., *op. cit.,* p. 7.

13. As Russell points out, "a frequent ground of objection to Newton's 'absolute' time has been that it could not be observed. This objection . . . comes oddly from men who ask us to believe in electrons and protons and neutrons, quantum transitions in atoms, and what not, none of which can be observed." *Op. cit.,* p. 268.

14. Feigl, H. "Logical Empiricism", *op. cit.,* p. 12.

15. *Meditations on First Philosophy,* I, 21, trans. John Veitch. Roman numbers designate the Meditation; Arabic numbers designate the page in the Open Court edition of 1937.

16. *Ibid,* I, 22.

17. *Ibid,* VI, 86.

18. *Ibid,* VI, 86.

19. *Ibid,* IV, 63.

20. *Ibid,* I, 25.

21. *Ibid,* VI, 88.

22. *Ibid,* VI, 90.

23. *Ibid,* II, 30.

24. *Ibid,* III, 43.

25. *Ibid,* III, 53.

One of the criteria which Descartes proposes for evaluating the truth-character of ideas is "natural light." After making a statement which seems to him to be a defensible proposition, he appeals to "natural light" for its validation. But this validates nothing. It is itself a presupposition. "The conservation of a substance, in each moment of its duration" (III, 58) is a definition; yet Descartes regards it as a proposition whose truth is substantiated by its classification as a "dictate of the natural light," (III, 58) Every instance of Descartes' appeal to the "natural light" (III, 62) is a case of restating, in other words a definition or a presupposition. This is obvious in the statement that "it is manifest by the natural light that there must be as much reality in the efficient and total cause as in its effect; for whence can the effect draw its reality if not from its cause." (III, 49) What Descartes regards as a certitude substantiated by natural light is upon an analysis seen to be no more than a definition. It is affirmed that there is no effect in excess of its cause. Hence, there must "be as much reality in the . . . cause as in its effect." But this is purely a restatement of a definition. Another instance of "all the other truths I discern by the natural light" is that "what is done cannot be undone." (VI, 96) This is purely an analytic statement: it is a stipulation of how a word is used.

There are other instances in which Descartes appeals to the "natural light" to authenticate a belief whose statement may be regarded as a real proposition, and not merely as an analytic statement. It is the affirmation that "the knowledge of the understanding ought always to precede the determination of the will." (IV, 71) This is the basic presupposition of a rationalistic moral philosophy. But to affirm that "it is a dictate of the natural light" (IV, 71) simply dodges the issue whether this statement is warranted in the light of the data it is supposed to interpret. Rationalistic moral philosophies assume that it is true. But there are others which do not. Thus it is presumptuous to appeal to a criterion of the "natural light" with a certitude that whatever one regards as an instance of it is, therefore, true. The circularity is obvious.

The most absurd of all such attempts to resolve a philosophical problem is Descartes' unsupported affirmation that "I am . . . clearly taught by the natural light that ideas exist in me as pictures or images." (III, 51) The very problem which gave rise to the *Meditations* is the perplexity whether there are ideas which inform of realities other than ideas. Here Descartes merely affirms that this is indisputable, and so is no problem. If its indisputability can be so easily established, the undertaking, in the first place, was a waste of time.

26. Descartes is a sound empiricist when he declares that "because I was in existence a short time ago, it does not follow that I must now exist". (III, 58) It would be preferable to restate this: because there is a thinking experience which is followed by another thinking experience, it may not be inferred that these two experiences have any necessary continuity. If there were a continuity in the experiences, this continuity would not be claimed as knowledge, since by definition of the initial thesis of strict empiricism, what is known is the immediately given. The immediately given is the experience from which nothing whatever is inferred, and for its existence nothing whatever is presupposed. The experience itself is the given, and is the object which is known in experience. It is, therefore, indefensible to affirm, as Descartes does, "I . . . know that I exist". (II, 34) This much cannot be claimed as knowledge. What is warranted, however, is that if the self is thinking, and if there is thinking, then there is a self. But this is only by definition that there is a self. Yet, Descartes does offer a definition of the self which is consistent with strict empiricism when he says, "nothing besides thinking belongs to the essence of the mind" (Preface to the Reader, p. 10). If this is really what he means, thinking is an experience which may be designated by the term "mind". But this is obviously not what Descartes intends to affirm.

He argues that "it cannot be that when *I* see, or which comes to the same thing, when *I* think *I* see, I myself who think am nothing". (III, 42) But this is no argument. It is an affirmation that there is a self which thinks. Yet the whole problem for Descartes is an analysis of the warrant for making this claim to knowledge that there is a self.

Hence, as stated, this is a begging of the question. The statement amounts to the affirmation that there is a self, and this self sees and thinks.

But the warrant for affirming this belief is the problem which Descartes proposes to examine. The affirmation "I am certain that I am a thinking thing" (III, 42) settles the whole issue. If there is warrant for this affirmation, then there is nothing more to analyze. The analysis has been made unnecessary by the dogmatism with which the claim to certain knowledge is made.

Descartes began his reflections with presuppositions, and he never succeeded in suspending these. His proposal to suspend them, and to confine his claims to knowledge to the immediately given evidence is only a proposal. He never remained consistent with the proposal. The very statement that "I am . . . assured that . . . perceptions and imaginations exist in me" (III, 42) is an example of the unexamined presupposition that there is a self which has experiences, and the experiences are other than its reality. They are, in other words, "modes" of the self. (III, 42; VI, 92)

Descartes declares that "thinking . . . alone is inseparable from me". (II, 33) This may be construed as a definition. When there is thinking, there is a self. But the self is the thinking, provided the claim is consistent with the initial statement that knowledge is of the immediately given. Thinking exists. This much is the given. But from this given, it does not follow that there is a self which is more than the experience of thinking.

Every definition of the self which Descartes offers is a *petitio principii*: "I do not observe that aught necessarily belongs to my nature or essence beyond my being a thinking thing". (VI, 91) After the repeated affirmations that he is a self which exists and has experiences, it is hardly necessary to prolong the argument further in order to find some belief which may be affirmed with certainty. He is certain that there is more than the immediate experience. This certainty means that he is not an empiricist, and hence, should not have proposed to limit his analysis to the conditions which are consistent with the thesis of strict empiricism.

He does not begin his analysis with thinking as the given. He begins it with the belief that when there is thinking, there is a self which thinks. This is a perfectly defensible point of view, but it is rather absurd to make the pompous claim that everything will be doubted except the thinking or the doubting, and then smuggle in one certitude after another, and leave them all unexamined.

He argues that he is a thinking being because he regards himself as a thinking being: "it is absolutely necessary to conclude from this alone that I am." (III, 61) By this circular statement, existence is inferred from the certainty that there is existence. It would be difficult to find a clearer statement of the Stoics' "irresistible impression" than this. The mind or the thinking self, is not itself directly apprehended. What is immediately experienced is the thinking experience. Hence it is indefensible to affirm that "I readily discover that there is nothing more . . . clearly apprehended than my own mind." (II, 41)

If "mind" for Descartes means nothing more than the experience of thinking, then this statement is warranted. But this is not his notion of the reality of the self. For him, there is a self which thinks. The thinking is its essence, but its essence is not to be equated with *an* act of thinking, or *a* thinking experience. Yet, according to the empirical thesis, the thinking is the reality of which there is certitude: not the reality of a thinker which is other than the thinking experience.

After affirming that "no one will ever be able to bring it about that I am not, so long as I shall be conscious that I am, or at any future time cause it to be that I have never been, *it being now true that I am*", (III, 44) there is nothing left to argue.

If this much is a warranted claim to knowledge on the evidence of the experience of thinking, then almost anything may be inferred from the thinking which is other than the experience itself.

The statement that nothing "necessarily belongs to my nature or essence beyond my being a thinking thing" (VI, 91) is a definition. Yet, Descartes declares that from this he "rightly conclude(s) that (his) essence consists only in (his) being a thinking thing". This, however, is no conclusion. It is merely a restatement of the original definition. This second statement is not even an inference. It is merely a verbal alternative to the first statement.

27. Descartes' statement that the "mind is . . . really distinct from the body" is a metaphysical presupposition. The statement that the body and mind are "so closely conjoined . . . as together to form, *as it were* a unity" (I, 19) affirms that the idea of their common character is after all only a fiction. Thus, what is not differentiated within experience, is differentiated when experience is interpreted by a dualistic presupposition. But this is reading into experience what one presupposes underlies experience. That their common character is not a feature of experience, but only a fiction in interpretation, certainly makes Descartes sound like Vaihinger. If it is only a fiction, it raises another very perplexing problem.

The problem is, if some of our ideas are only fictions, and others are not, just how are we to distinguish between ideas which are fictional and those which inform us of the nature of some reality existing apart from ideas? It is dogmatism to maintain that all our ideas are fictions. It is equally dogmatic to maintain that all our ideas inform us of a reality which is external to ideas. It is less dogmatic to affirm that some of our ideas *may* inform us of a reality which may exist external to our ideas.

But all three positions are presuppositions. The third presupposition is the one which persists in the thinking of Descartes, although his

NOTES

dogmatic dualistic metaphysic is inconsistent with such a belief.

28. Descartes declares "I embrace in thought . . . the representation of the object". (III, 45) This presupposition he affirms as an instance of "natural light". (III, 51)

No theory of knowledge can be formulated without presuppositions. A critical philosophy, however, enumerates these presuppositions. An uncritical philosophy isn't aware that they are presuppositions.

There are seven specific presuppositions unacknowledged as presuppositions in the single statement which Descartes offers as a warranted claim to knowledge: "On the ground that God is no deceiver, and that consequently he has permitted no falsity in my opinions which he has not likewise given me a faculty of correcting, I think I may with safety conclude that I possess in myself the means of arriving at the truth." (VI, 93)

What Descartes calls a conclusion is only another presupposition in addition to the other that (i) there is a God; (ii) this God does not deceive; (iii) man's capacities for experience are created by this God who does not deceive; (iv) some uses of these capacities are as God intended them to be used; (v) what Descartes believes to be true, is true; (vi) an individual's estimate of a true belief is itself a true belief; (vii) Descartes knows that the nature of God is as he believes it is.

By the circular character of his argument, he dodges the entire problem of a critical theory of knowledge. He declares that "it . . . follows . . . that I can never, therefore be deceived for if all I possess be from God, and if he planted in me no faculty that is deceitful, it seems to follow that I can never fall into error". (IV, 64) This is a syllogistic conclusion from two premises which are unexamined presuppositions. They are affirmed as certain, and hence the conclusion follows that he has a belief of which he may be certain. But the truth-character of this analytical conclusion from the two premises is purely formal. The real problem for scrutiny is not the consistency of the conclusion from the premises, but the warrant for the premises. The warrant for the premises is the concern which motivated his analysis.

But Descartes' analysis of his beliefs is simply an enumeration of all the beliefs he maintains during his analysis. Every analysis of experience begins with presuppositions. A philosophically sound analysis, however, is an enumeration of the beliefs which constitute the presuppositions in the analysis.

29. *Ibid,* Synopsis, 16.
30. *Ibid,* V, 77 (underlining mine).
31. *Ibid,* V, 77.
32. *Ibid,* Synopsis, 18.
33. *Ibid,* V, 79.
34. In his *Proslogium* (Ch. II) Saint Anselm declares "we believe that thou art a being than which nothing greater can be conceived."

154

NOTES

This statement affirms a belief in the reality of God: it does not affirm an inference of the reality of God from the definition of God. This therefore is not the so-called ontological argument. God is defined as "a being than which nothing greater can be conceived", and the reality of such a being which is affirmed.

Anselm, however, proposes to demonstrate the necessity for God's existence from the definition of God's existence. This is the so-called ontological argument. It is "that than which nothing greater can be conceived cannot exist in the understanding alone. For, suppose it exists in the understanding alone: then it can be conceived to exist in reality: which is greater. Therefore, if that, than which nothing greater can be conceived, exists in the understanding alone, the very being, than which nothing greater can be conceived, is one, than which a greater can be conceived. But this is impossible. Hence, there is no doubt that there exists a being, than which nothing greater can be conceived, and it exists both in the understanding and in reality." But in criticism of this argument, it must be pointed out that the idea of God's existence as that which is other than the idea of his existence is still the idea of his existence as other than the idea of his existence.

35. *Ibid*, V, 79.

36. *Religion Within the Limits of Reason Alone,* p. 66. Open Court, Chicago, 1934. Trans. T. M. Greene and H. Hudson.

37. *The Christian Faith,* p. 193. Scribners, Edinburgh, 1928.
As Professor H. R. Mackintosh says, "If words mean anything, doctrine is for (Schleiermacher) a statement about our feeling, not about God." *Types of Modern Theology,* p. 66. "Dogmatic (for Schleiermacher) . . . would consist exclusively, to use his fatal phrase, in 'descriptions of human states'". p. 67. "All attributes which we ascribe to God are to be taken as denoting not something specific in God, but only something specific in the manner in which the feeling of absolute dependence is to be related to Him." *Christian Faith,* para. 50.

38. *Ibid,* para. 3 and 4.

39. So consistent is Schleiermacher's analysis of religious faith a psychology of experience, rather than a theology of the nature of a divine reality transcendent of experience, that he even admits, as Professor Mackintosh points out, "the idea of God is irrelevant for religion: true faith can dispense with it altogether." (*Op. cit.,* p. 51) "In the *Addresses* he has been emphatic that piety may exist without any idea of God whatsoever: but in the *Dogmatic* apparently moving on a step, he lays down that God means 'the Whence of our receptive and active existence.'" *Op. cit.,* p. 64.

As Professor Mackintosh points out, "you can only speak of faith where there is a Word of God on which faith rests". p. 68. But "Schleiermacher's eye . . . was bent on inward facts, as though the soul could feed on its own vitals". p. 68. "This tenacious vein of psychologism in

155

Schleiermacher is a prejudice and disability that haunts his *Dogmatic* from the first page to the last. He can even declare that 'nothing is *given* us except the souls in which we light upon the pious affections' ". p. 67-8.

40. "A kindred ambiguity, and one equally rich in fallacies, has often in later theologies come to attach to the term 'experience'." p. 48.
41. *Confessions of St. Augustine*, Book IX.

Chapter Six

1. *Prolegomena*, p. 43.
2. *Ibid*, p. 48.
3. Russell says that canons of inductive inference "are valid if the world has certain characteristics which we all believe it to have." *Op. cit.*, p. 496.
4. Russell points out that "an atom only gives evidence of its existence when it emits energy, and therefore experimental evidence can only be of changes of energy." *Ibid*, p. 23.
   C. I. Lewis says that "The existence of electrons is inferred from the behavior of oil-droplets between charged plates." "Experience and Meaning," p. 139, *Readings in Philosophical Analysis*.

Chapter Seven

1. *Essay Concerning Human Understanding*, II, I, 10.
2. Pap, A., *Elements of Analytic Philosophy*, p. 403.
3. Jeans says that "The Model works well for a time and then suddenly breaks in our hands. In the new light of the wave-mechanics, the hard sphere is seen to be hopelessly inadequate to represent the electron." *The Universe Around Us*, p. 129. Cambridge University Press, 1929.
4. W. H. Werkmeister maintains that the "formula is the *concept* . . . knowing the structure formula, we know what type of reactions may be expected." *The Basis and Structure of Knowledge*, p. 56. Harper and Brothers, N. Y., 1948.

Chapter Eight

1. Reichenbach proposes that "meaning is a predicate of propositions" (p. 20, 28) and "sense" is a predicate of words, ("words have sense"), (p. 20). Yet, he nevertheless says that symbols "have a meaning". *Experience and Prediction*, p. 27, The University of Chicago Press, Chicago, 1938.
2. *Meditations*, "Synopsis of the Six Following Meditations", p. 16.
3. *Ibid*, Bk. III, p. 58.
4. *Proslogium*, Ch. II.

NOTES

Chapter Nine

1. *Essay Concerning Human Understanding*, IV, 1, 2.
2. *Human Knowledge*, p. 26.
3. *Essay Concerning Human Understanding*, II, XXIII, 6.
4. Eddington, A., *New Pathways in Science*, p. 210. Macmillan, N. Y., 1935.
5. *Op. cit.*, II, 1, 10
6. *Confessions*, p. 83.
7. *Op. cit.*, p. 115.
8. "The reality of the divine requires no proof," says Boodin, "any more than the existence of the external physical world or of our fellow-men . . . and . . . it cannot be proved . . . Life always turns out to be a venture of faith." *God*, p. 27. Macmillan, N. Y., 1934.
9. *Op. cit.*, p. 116.
10. These "premises" are, as Feigl declares, "assumptions, ever ready for revision, valid only 'until further notice'." "The Logical Character of Induction", p. 303, *Readings in Philosophical Analysis*.

    As Morris declares, "many of our practices for which we invoke the sanction of science—including some techniques in contemporary science itself—will be regarded by later generations as magical. This is a special instance of the general point that a person may be mistaken as to the type of discourse which he is producing or interpreting." *Signs, Language, and Behavior*, p. 144. Prentice Hall, N. Y., 1946.

Chapter Ten

1. *Phaedrus*, 247, 248.
2. *John* 9:16.
3. Brunner, E., *Philosophy of Religion*, p. 179. Nicholson and Watson, London, 1937.
4. *Ibid*, p. 179.
5. *Matthew* 10, 16.
6. Brunner, E., *op. cit.*, p. 171.
7. *Summa Theologica*, Q. 1, Art. 6.
8. Brunner, E., *op. cit.*, p. 180.
9. *Romans* 1:20.
10. Brunner, E., *op. cit.*, p. 22.
11. *Ibid*, p. 151.
12. *Ibid*, p. 17
13. Otto, R., *op. cit.*, p. 178.
14. *John* 17:21.
15. Kant, I., *Religion Within the Limits of Reason Alone*, p. 94.
16. Wobbermin, G., *The Nature of Religion*, p. 25, Crowell, N. Y., 1933.

INDEX

A

abstraction, 52, 125, 145
Academy, 21
acceleration, 90, 92
acquaintance, 33
analysis, 29, 52, 71, 81, 99, 101
analyst, 5, 10, 55
analytical statement, 65
Anselm, St., 67, 109
anthropomorphic, 95
appearance, 73
a priori, 31, 35
Aquinas, St. Thomas, 9, 132, 139, 140
argument, 108
Aristotle, 4, 21, 122
assumption, 7, 29, 33, 36, 59, 61, 62,
    75, 76, 78, 80, 81, 83, 86, 89, 101,
    104, 109, 111, 112, 123, 126, 127,
    128, 130
astronomy, 4, 88, 118
atomic structure 77ff, 94, 121, 122
Augustine, St., 12, 131
awareness, 100

B

Bohr, N., 94, 95
Boyle, R., 91
Brunner, E., 136, 141, 142

C

calculus, 3, 20, 25, 27
causal, 80
causation, 39, 40, 73, 74
caution, 117

Christian, 140, 144
circular, 90, 130, 132, 138
classification, 117, 127
cognition, 30
cognitive function, 55, 58
concept, 34, 50
confidence, 115
conjunctive, 17
consistency, 26, 32, 99, 144
construct, 89, 93, 96, 97
context, 105
convention, 25, 27
Conventionalism, 23
Copernicus, N., 4
corrections, 90, 115
correlation, 80, 82, 86, 91, 102, 112,
    126, 132
correspondence, 26
credibility, 92, 111, 112
creed, 57
criterion, 72, 99, 112, 134, 135ff, 142,
    143, 145

D

deduction, 25, 26, 80
definition, 65
demonstration, 68
Descartes, R., 1, 61-64, 67, 107, 108,
    109
description, 100, 101, 102, 118
designation, 6, 14, 15, 18, 23, 24, 50,
    53, 96, 98, 106, 115
Dionysius, 51
divine purpose, 90, 91, 92, 93, 132
divine reality, 26, 46, 52, 54, 68, 76,
    95, 97, 106, 107, 108, 110, 117, 131,

159

INDEX

134, 135, 137, 139, 143, 144, 146

dogmatism, 7, 21, 23, 31, 35, 50, 69, 74, 103

dualism, 32, 49, 53, 74

E

electron, 79

empirical analysis, 40, 55, 66, 67, 98, 127

empirical grounds, 31, 32, 38

empirical method, 102

empirical test, 59, 130

Empiricism, 34, 37, 40, 56, 58, 63, 77, 103

empiricist position, 8, 33, 62, 73, 74, 75, 82, 83, 98, 99, 113, 121, 127

equivalence, 108

Euclid, 3

Euclidean geometry, 35

evaluation, 112

excluded middle, 14, 16

existence, 10

experience, 32, 33, 34, 37, 62-65, 73-76

expressibility, 5

F

faith, 27, 50, 57, 65, 71, 75, 77, 78, 109, 120, 126, 127, 128, 129, 132, 133, 135, 140, 143, 144

Feuerbach L., 105, 106

Fichte, J. G., 53

formal logic, 18

formal system, 1, 20, 25, 26

G

galaxy, 87

Galileo, 90, 91

Galileo's law, 89

generalization, 91

geometry, 3

God, 27, 47, 68, 70, 88, 106, 107, 109, 132, 142, 143

grammar, 5, 14, 18, 23, 24, 28

H

Hobbes, T., 56

Hume, D., 35, 39, 40, 68, 120, 126

hypothesis, 37, 38, 79, 87, 89, 90, 92, 111, 112, 113, 115, 117, 119, 120, 122, 123, 124, 125, 126, 128, 131

I

ideal, 106, 124, 125

ideal context, 90, 125, 126

identity, 15, 16, 127

inconsistency, 16, 73

induction, 60, 81, 82

inference, 17, 75, 78, 79, 86, 101

information, 84, 116, 118

informative value, 61, 65, 110, 112, 128

insight, 31

interpretation, 7, 12, 17, 19, 20, 25, 37, 43, 50, 59, 60, 65, 73, 77, 85, 88, 89, 93, 94, 96, 104, 106, 115, 116, 123, 124, 125, 127, 131, 134, 142, 146

interpretative function, 111

J

Jeans, J., 41-43

Jesus, 135, 138, 140, 143

judgment, 5, 103, 108, 129, 138

K

Kant, I., 27, 30, 31, 32, 33, 34, 37, 38, 47, 54, 69, 73, 74, 145

knowledge, 26, 27, 29, 36, 43, 80, 82, 101, 113, 116, 117, 121, 128, 133, 140

knowledge-claims, 8, 12, 27, 28, 30, 35, 39, 43, 44, 47, 54, 64, 66, 70, 76, 77, 98, 100, 107, 114, 118, 127, 134

INDEX

referential function, 62, 65
relations, 85
religion, 57
religious experience, 52, 70
religious faith, 27, 48, 50, 53, 68, 69, 70, 71, 92, 110
religious individual, 91, 132
religious institutions, 57, 136, 143
religious interpretation, 26, 50, 132, 133
religious life, 57, 97, 117, 134, 136, 137, 143, 144
religious significance, 24, 47
Renaissance, 68
reverence, 96
Richards, I. A., 12, 56
Russell, B., 11

S

Santayana, G., 27
Schleiermacher, F., 69, 70, 71
Schopenhauer, A., 53
science, 82, 96, 117, 119, 124, 126, 128, 129, 130
scientific knowledge, 41, 43
selection, 91, 130, 139
sensation, 74
sense, 25, 26
sensory data, 120, 121, 123, 124, 125, 127, 132
sensory experience, 35, 61, 64, 76, 78, 80, 85, 89, 117, 119, 126
serial order, 98
sign, 95
significance, 1, 98, 106, 133
Skepticism, 63, 82
space, perceptual, 80
space, physical, 80
spatial pattern, 31
stars, 85, 122
Subjectivism, 27
substitution, 1, 145
symbol, 1, 9, 25, 26, 95, 97, 98, 102, 104, 106

symbolic device, 105
symbolic function, 94, 95, 106
Symbolic Logic, 8, 9
symbolic procedure, 107
symbolic reference, 95
symbolic system, 16
symbolic techniques, 8
symbolism, 2, 3, 104
synthetic statement, 65

T

tautology, 17
tenacity, 115
terminology, 84, 104
theology, 2, 53, 54, 55, 56, 58, 70, 71, 72, 110, 142
theory of knowledge, 29, 69, 70, 100, 102
thinkability, 4
truth, 19, 77
truth-character, 17, 24, 43, 72, 136, 139, 142, 143

U

understanding, 34, 142
universe, 87, 123, 125
Uranus, 120

V

vacuum, 90
validity, 145
verbal statement, 55
verbal system, 56
verification, 90

W

warrant, 30, 77, 78, 81, 84, 99, 101, 127, 128, 129, 130, 134, 138
warrantability, 5, 127
Whitehead, A. N., 12
Wobbermin, G., 145